GUITAR RECORDED VERSIONS

NEIL YOUNG
WITH CRAZY HORSE
EVERYBODY KNOWS
THIS IS NOWHERE

CONTENTS

MUSIC TRANSCRIPTIONS BY JEFF JACOBSON AND KEVIN LANGAN
ISBN: 978-1-4234-9083-8

HAL•LEONARD®
CORPORATION
7777 W. BLUEMOUND RD. P.O. BOX 13819 MILWAUKEE, WI 53213

Ralph Molina

Billy Talbot

Danny Whitten

CINNAMON GIRL

I WANT TO LIVE WITH A CINNAMON GIRL
I COULD BE HAPPY THE REST OF MY LIFE
WITH A CINNAMON GIRL

A DREAMER OF PICTURES
I RUN IN THE NIGHT
YOU SEE US TOGETHER
CHASING THE MOONLIGHT
MY CINNAMON GIRL

TEN SILVER SAXES
A BASS WITH A BOW
THE DRUMMER RELAXES
AND WAITS BETWEEN SHOWS
FOR HIS CINNAMON GIRL

A DREAMER OF PICTURES
I RUN IN THE NIGHT
YOU SEE US TOGETHER
CHASING THE MOONLIGHT
MY CINNAMON GIRL

MA SEND ME MONEY NOW
I'M GONNA MAKE IT SOMEHOW
I NEED ANOTHER CHANCE
YOU SEE YOUR BABY LOVES TO DANCE
YEAH
YEAH
YEAH

Cinnamon Girl

Words and Music by Neil Young

Verse

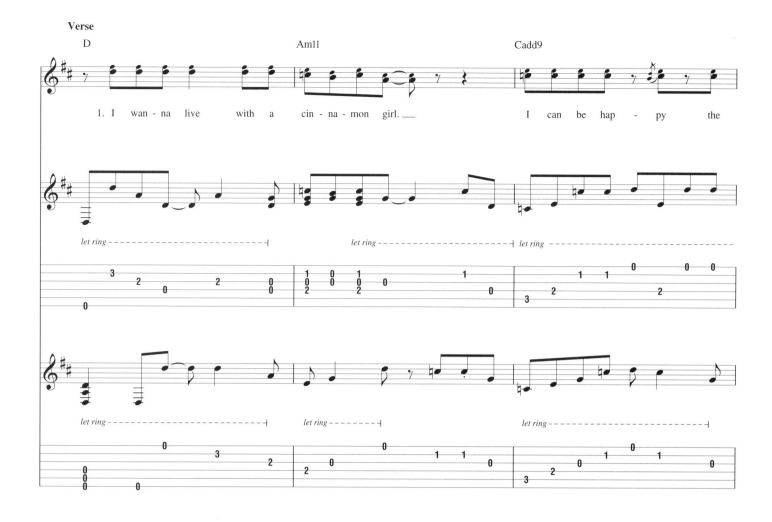

1. I wan-na live with a cin-na-mon girl. ___ I can be hap - py the

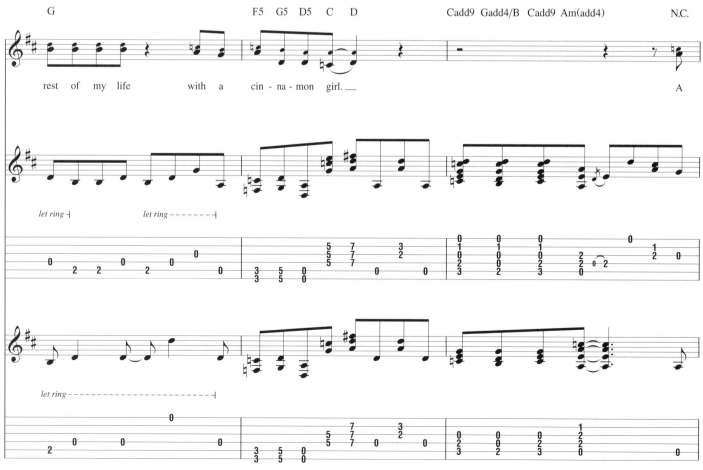

rest of my life with a cin-na-mon girl. ___

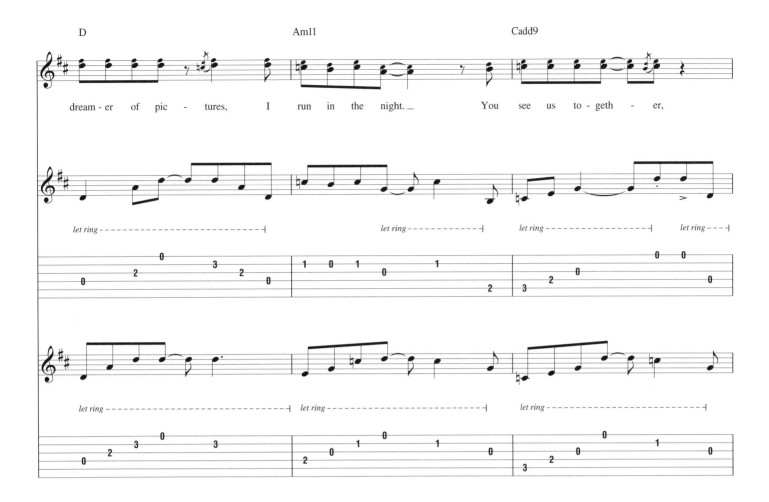

dream - er of pic - tures, I run in the night. ___ You see us to - geth - er,

chas - ing the moon - light, ___ my cin - na - mon girl. ___

Interlude

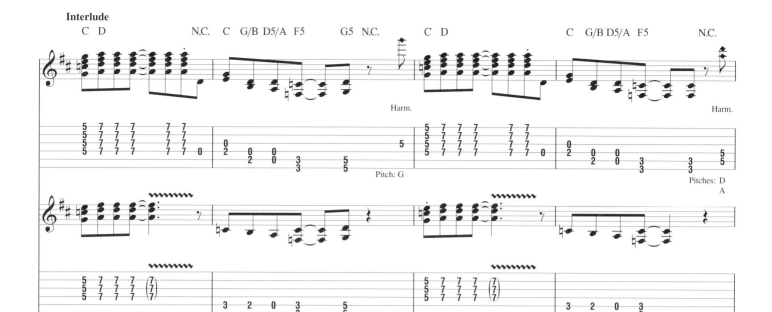

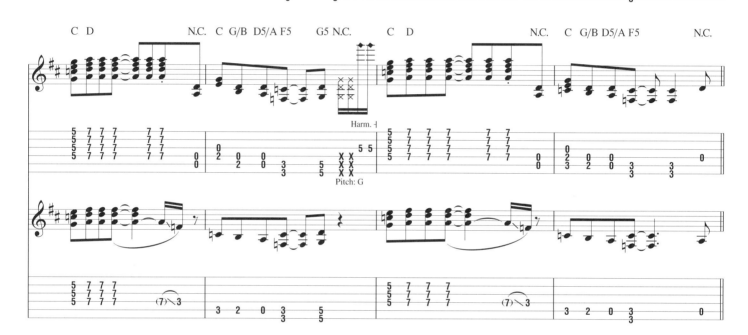

Verse

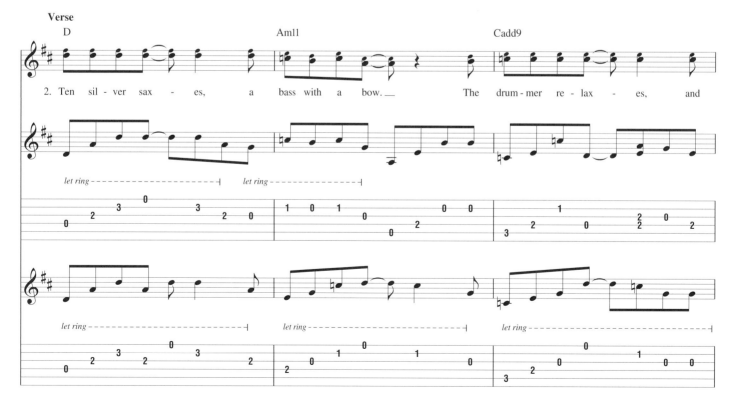

2. Ten sil - ver sax - es, a bass with a bow. The drum - mer re - lax - es, and

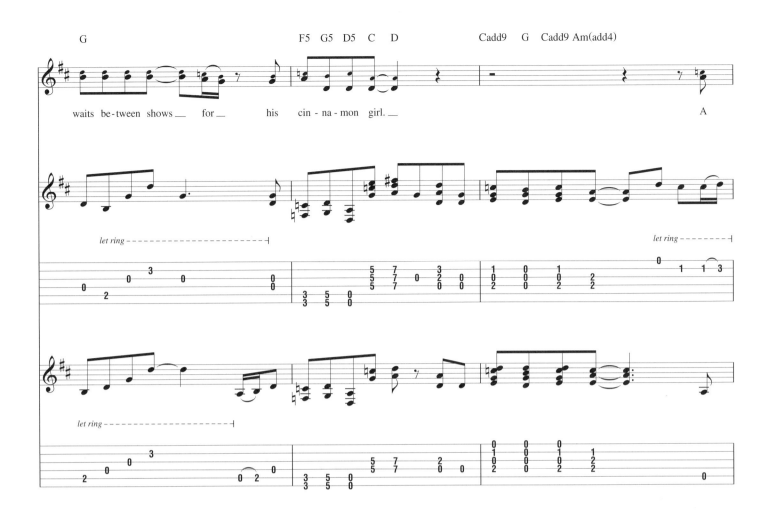

waits be-tween shows __ for __ his cin - na - mon girl. __

A

dream - er of pic - tures, I run in the night. __ You see us to - geth - er,

chas - ing the moon - light, ___ my cin - na - mon girl. ___

Interlude

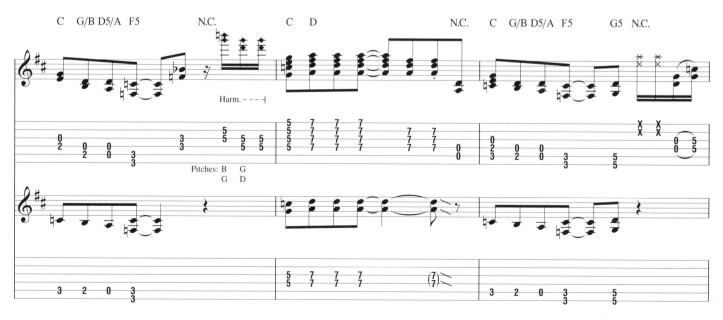

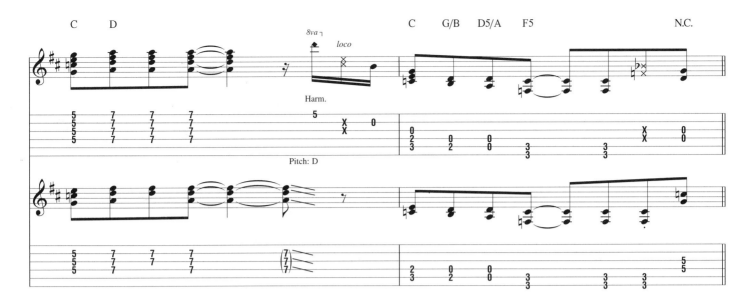

Bridge

Pa, send me mon - ey now, ___ I'm gon - na make it some - how, ___ I need an - oth - er chance. ___

You see your ba - by loves to dance! ___ Yeah! ___ Yeah! ___ Yeah! ___
(dance!) ___

Guitar Solo

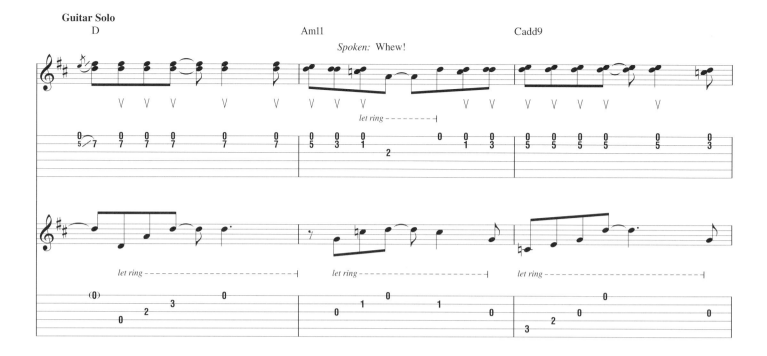

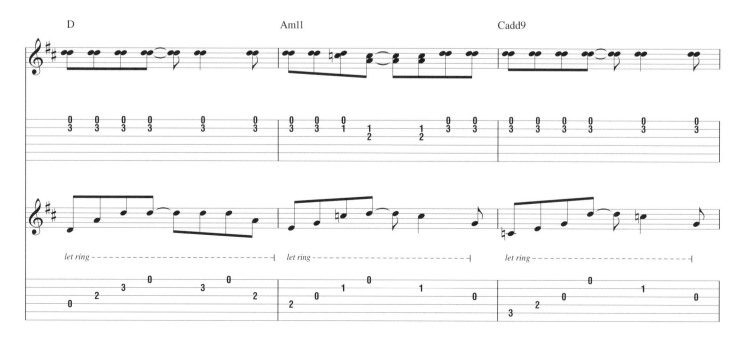

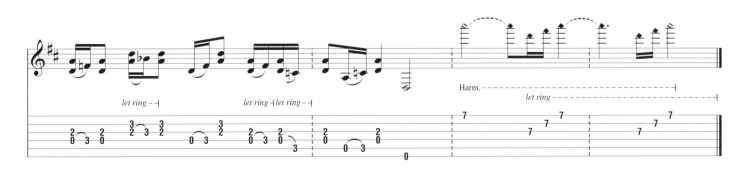

EVERYBODY KNOWS THIS IS NOWHERE

I THINK I'D LIKE TO GO BACK HOME
AND TAKE IT EASY
THERE'S A WOMAN THAT I'D LIKE TO GET TO KNOW
LIVING THERE
EVERYBODY SEEMS TO WONDER
WHAT IT'S LIKE DOWN HERE

I GOTTA GET AWAY FROM THIS DAY-TO-DAY RUNNIN' AROUND
EVERYBODY KNOWS THIS IS NOWHERE

EVERYBODY, EVERYBODY KNOWS
EVERYBODY KNOWS

EVERY TIME I THINK ABOUT BACK HOME
IT'S COOL AND BREEZY
I WISH THAT I COULD BE THERE RIGHT NOW
JUST PASSIN' TIME
EVERYBODY SEEMS TO WONDER
WHAT IT'S LIKE DOWN HERE

I GOTTA GET AWAY FROM THIS DAY-TO-DAY RUNNIN' AROUND
EVERYBODY KNOWS THIS IS NOWHERE

EVERYBODY, EVERYBODY KNOWS
EVERYBODY KNOWS

Everybody Knows This Is Nowhere

Words and Music by Neil Young

18

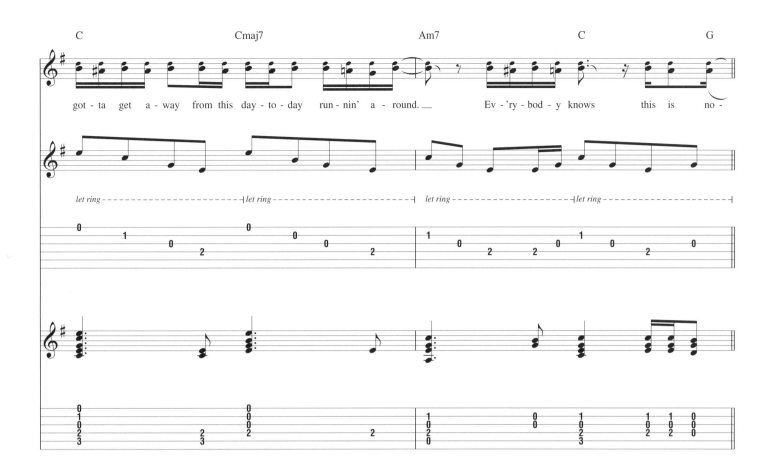

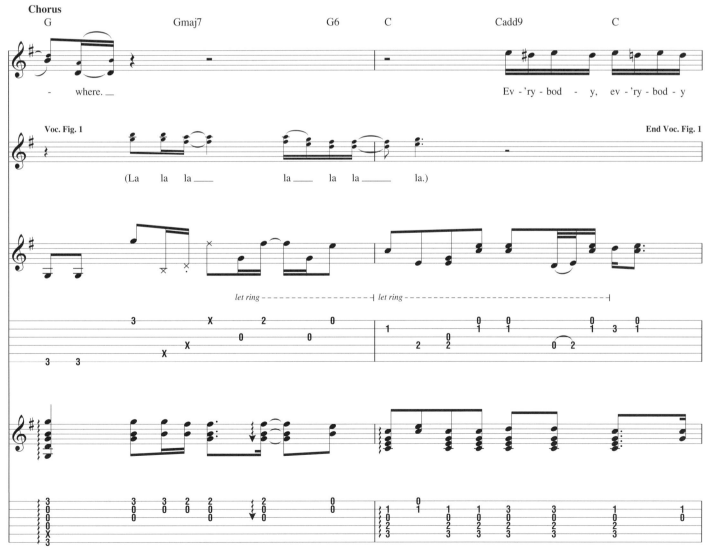

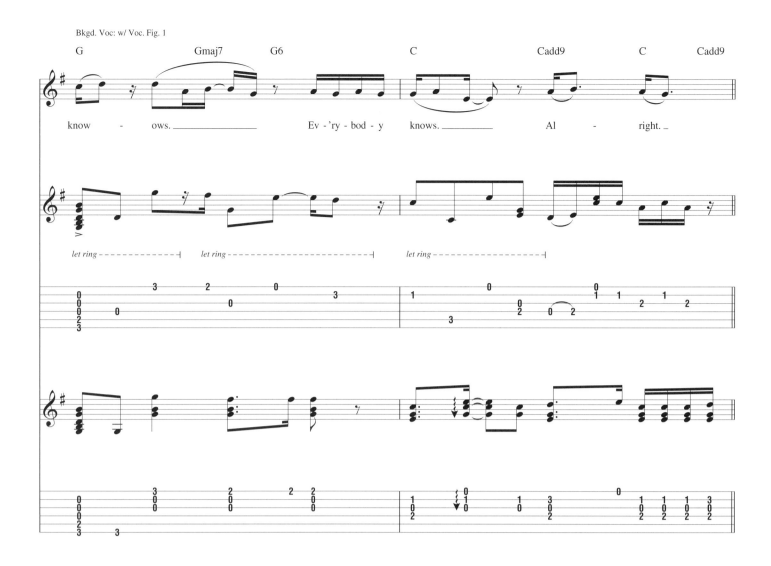

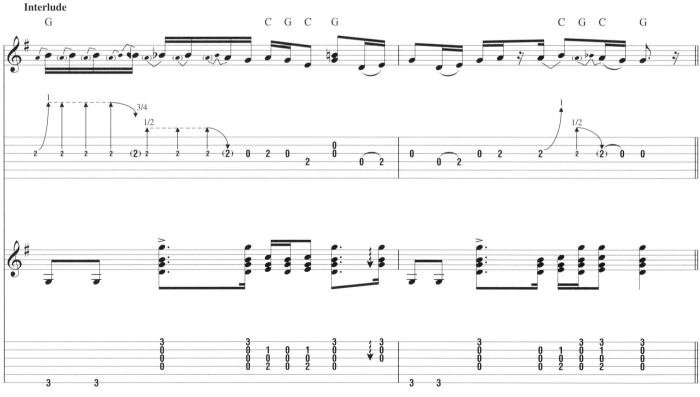

Verse

2. Ev-'ry time I think a-bout back home, __ it's cool __ and breez - y. __ I

wish that I could be there right now, __ just pass - in' time. ____

Ev-'ry-bod-y seems __ to won-der _____ what it's like down __ here.   I

got-ta get a-way from this day-to-day run-nin' a-round. __ Ev-'ry-bod-y knows __ this is no-

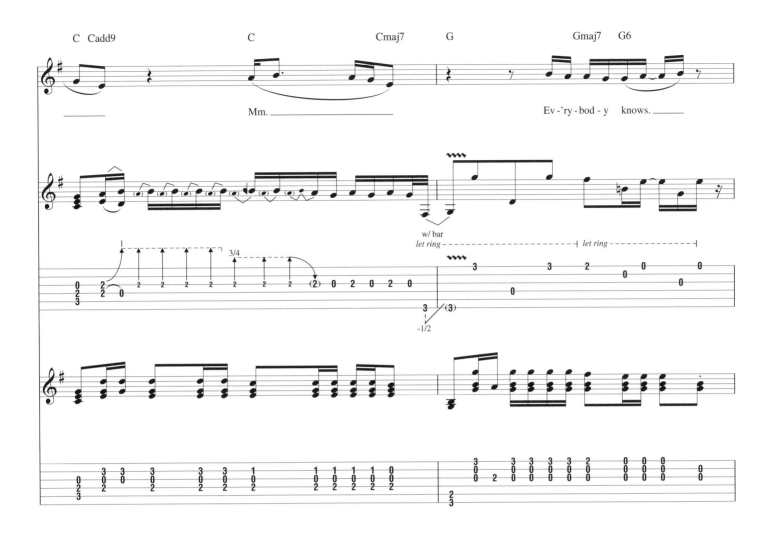

Outro-Guitar Solo
Begin fade

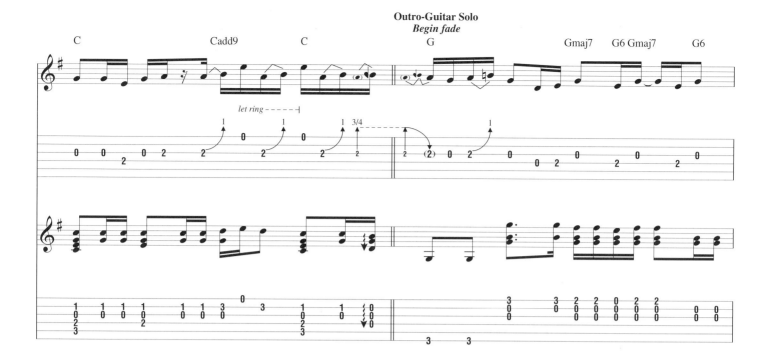

Fade out

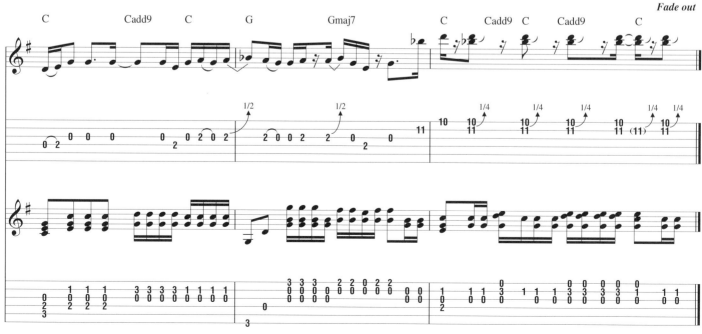

ROUND AND ROUND
(IT WON'T BE LONG)

ROUND AND ROUND AND ROUND WE SPIN
TO WEAVE A WALL TO HEM US IN
IT WON'T BE LONG, IT WON'T BE LONG

HOW SLOW AND SLOW AND SLOW IT GOES
TO MEND THE TEAR THAT ALWAYS SHOWS
IT WON'T BE LONG, IT WON'T BE LONG

IT'S HARD ENOUGH LOSING THE PAPER ILLUSION YOU'VE HIDDEN INSIDE
WITHOUT THE CONFUSION OF FINDING YOU'RE USING THE CRUTCH OF THE LIE
TO SHELTER YOUR PRIDE WHEN YOU CRY

ROUND AND ROUND AND ROUND WE SPIN
TO WEAVE A WALL TO HEM US IN
IT WON'T BE LONG, IT WON'T BE LONG

HOW SLOW AND SLOW AND SLOW IT GOES
TO MEND THE TEAR THAT ALWAYS SHOWS
IT WON'T BE LONG, IT WON'T BE LONG

NOW YOU'RE GROOVING TOO SLOW AND WHEREVER YOU GO THERE'S ANOTHER BESIDES
IT'S SO HARD TO SAY NO TO YOURSELF AND IT SHOWS THAT YOU'RE LOSING INSIDE
WHEN YOU STEP ON YOUR PRIDE AND YOU CRY

ROUND AND ROUND AND ROUND WE SPIN
TO WEAVE A WALL TO HEM US IN
IT WON'T BE LONG, IT WON'T BE LONG

HOW SLOW AND SLOW AND SLOW IT GOES
TO MEND THE TEAR THAT ALWAYS SHOWS
IT WON'T BE LONG, IT WON'T BE LONG

NOW THE HOURS WILL BEND THROUGH THE TIME THAT YOU SPEND TILL YOU TURN TO YOUR EYES
AND YOU SEE YOUR BEST FRIEND LOOKING OVER THE END AND YOU TURN TO SEE WHY
AND HE LOOKS IN YOUR EYES AND HE CRIES

ROUND AND ROUND AND ROUND WE SPIN
TO WEAVE A WALL TO HEM US IN
IT WON'T BE LONG, IT WON'T BE LONG

HOW SLOW AND SLOW AND SLOW IT GOES
TO MEND THE TEAR THAT ALWAYS SHOWS
IT WON'T BE LONG, IT WON'T BE LONG

Round & Round
(It Won't Be Long)

Words and Music by Neil Young

Gtr. 1 tacet

A

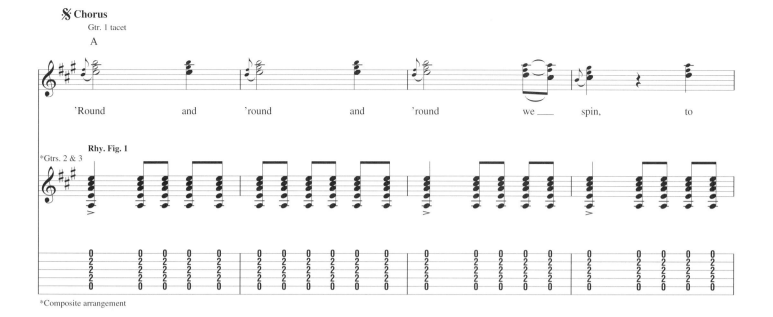

'Round   and   'round   and   'round   we ___ spin,   to

Rhy. Fig. 1

*Gtrs. 2 & 3

*Composite arrangement

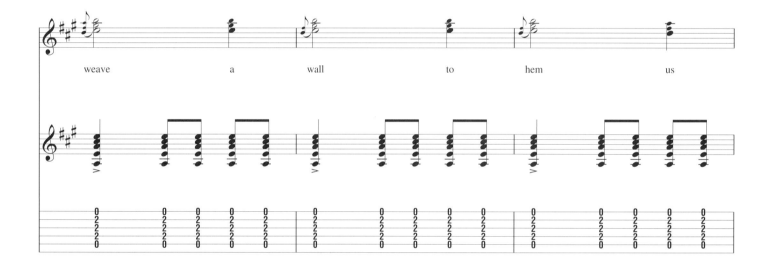

weave   a   wall   to   hem   us

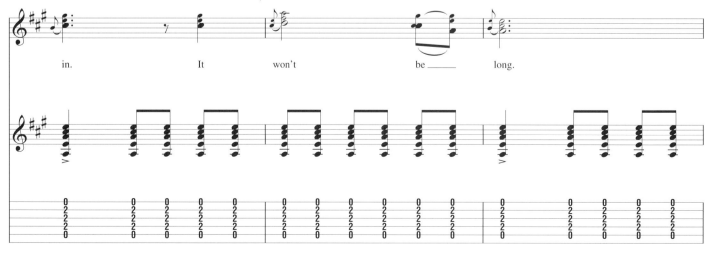

in.   It   won't   be ___ long.

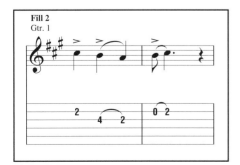

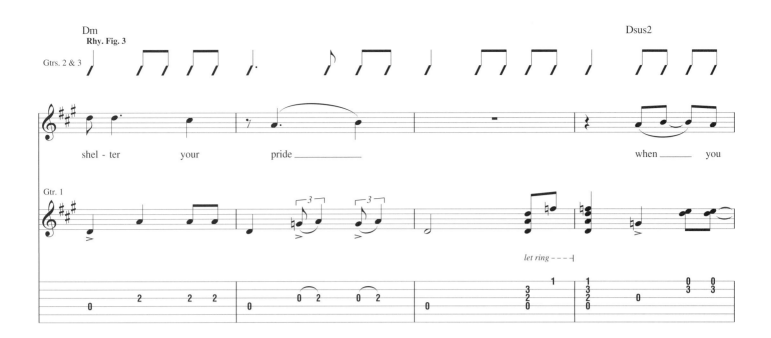

shel - ter   your   pride _____

when _____   you

D.S. al Coda 1

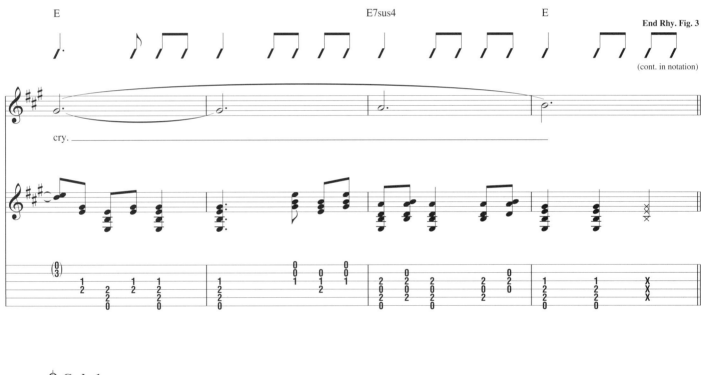

cry. _____

⊕ **Coda 1**
Verse
Bkgd. Voc: w/ Voc. Fig. 1
Gtrs. 2 & 3: w/ Rhy. Fig. 2 (2 times)

groov - in' too   slow,   and wher - ev - er   you go _____   there's an -

oth - er be - sides._____ It's so hard __ to say

no to your - self ____ and it shows that you're los - in' in - side _____

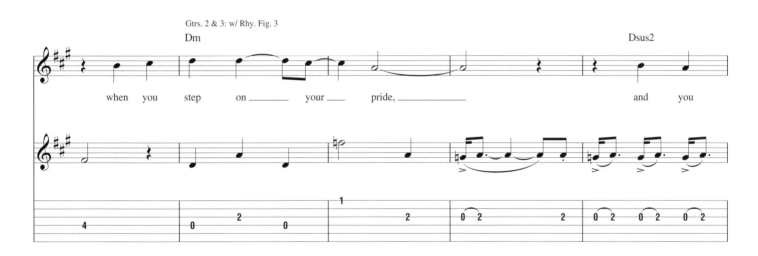

Gtrs. 2 & 3: w/ Rhy. Fig. 3

when you step on _____ your ___ pride, _____ and you

D.S. al Coda 2

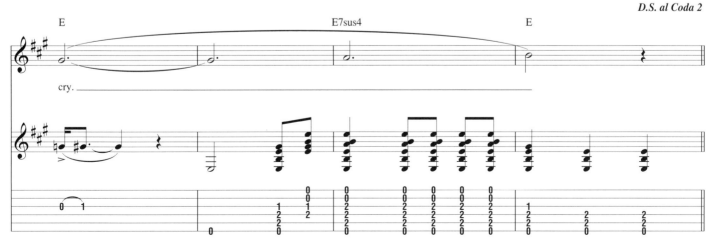

cry. _____

35

⊕ Coda 2

Verse

Bkgd. Voc: w/ Voc. Fig. 1
Gtrs. 2 & 3: w/ Rhy. Fig. 2 (2 times)

hours ___ will bend through the time that you spend till you turn to your

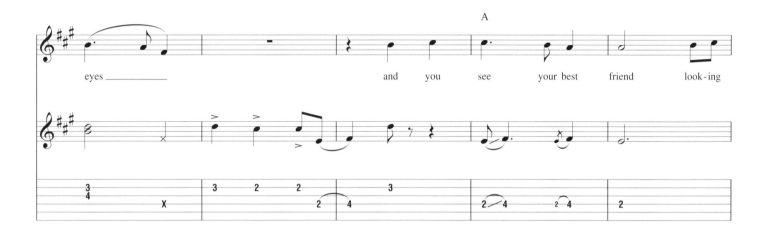

eyes ___ and you see your best friend look-ing

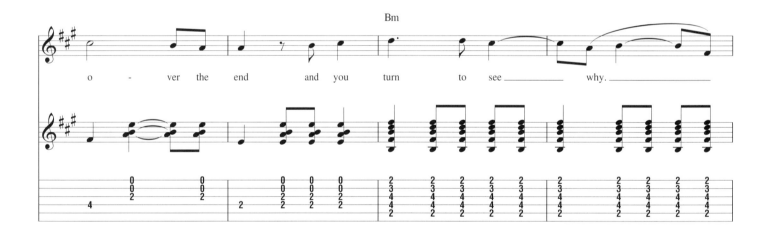

o - ver the end and you turn to see ___ why. ___

Gtrs. 2 & 3: w/ Rhy. Fig. 3

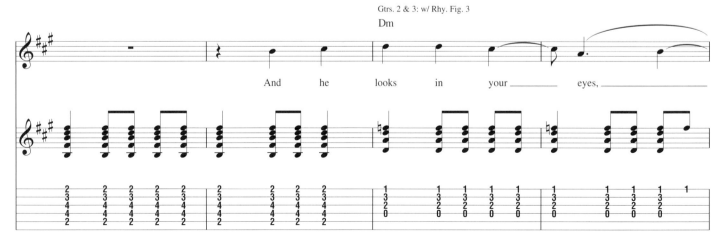

And he looks in your ___ eyes, ___

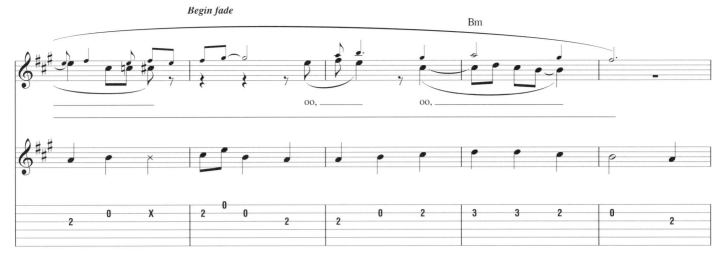

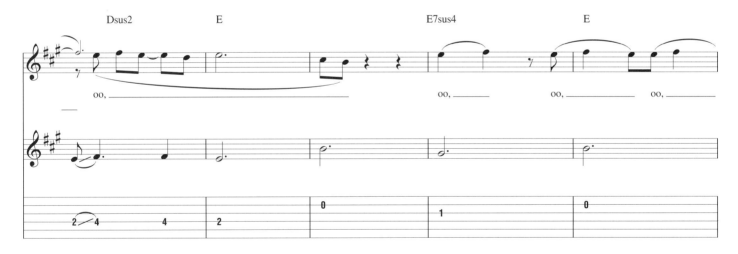

DOWN BY THE RIVER

BE ON MY SIDE, I'LL BE ON YOUR SIDE
THERE IS NO REASON FOR YOU TO HIDE
IT'S SO HARD FOR ME STAYING HERE ALL ALONE
WHEN YOU COULD BE TAKING ME FOR A RIDE
SHE COULD DRAG ME OVER THE RAINBOW
AND SEND ME AWAY

DOWN BY THE RIVER
I SHOT MY BABY
DOWN BY THE RIVER
DEAD
(OOH, SHOT HER DEAD)

YOU TAKE MY HAND, I'LL TAKE YOUR HAND
TOGETHER WE MAY GET AWAY
THIS MUCH MADNESS IS TOO MUCH SORROW
IT'S IMPOSSIBLE TO MAKE IT TODAY

SHE COULD DRAG ME OVER THE RAINBOW
AND SEND ME AWAY
DOWN BY THE RIVER
I SHOT MY BABY
DOWN BY THE RIVER
DEAD,
(DEAD, OOOH, OOOH
SHOT HER DEAD...SHOT HER DEAD)

BE ON MY SIDE, I'LL BE ON YOUR SIDE
THERE IS NO REASON FOR YOU TO HIDE
IT'S SO HARD FOR ME STAYING HERE ALL ALONE
WHEN YOU COULD BE TAKING ME FOR A RIDE

SHE COULD DRAG ME OVER THE RAINBOW
AND SEND ME AWAY
DOWN BY THE RIVER...I SHOT MY BABY
DOWN BY THE RIVER

(REPEAT)

Down by the River

Words and Music by Neil Young

*Chord symbols reflect basic harmony.
**Turn gtr.'s vol. knob down about half way to produce clean tone.

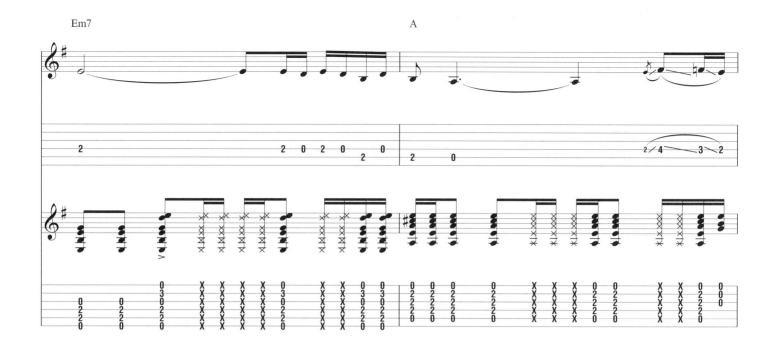

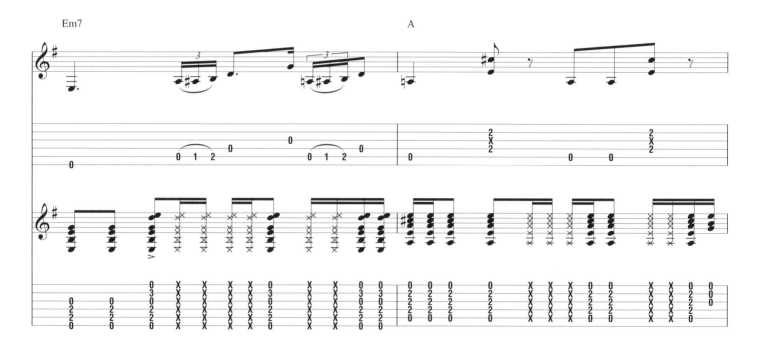

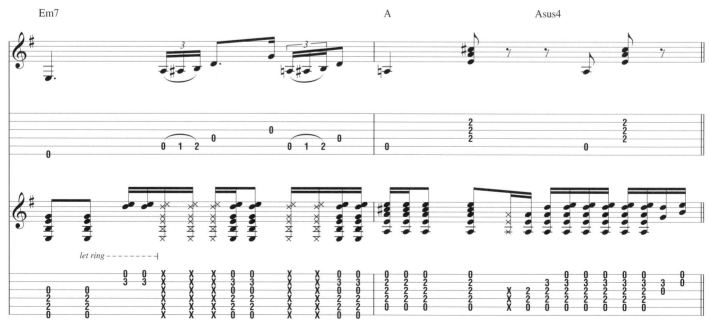

2nd time, Gtrs. 1 & 2: w/ Rhy. Figs. 2 & 2A

1. Be on my ___ side, I'll be on your ___ side, ___ ba - by. }
3. Be on my ___ side, I'll be on your ___ side. ___

There is ___ no rea - son ___ for you ___ to hide. ___

*1st time, this meas. sung behind the beat.

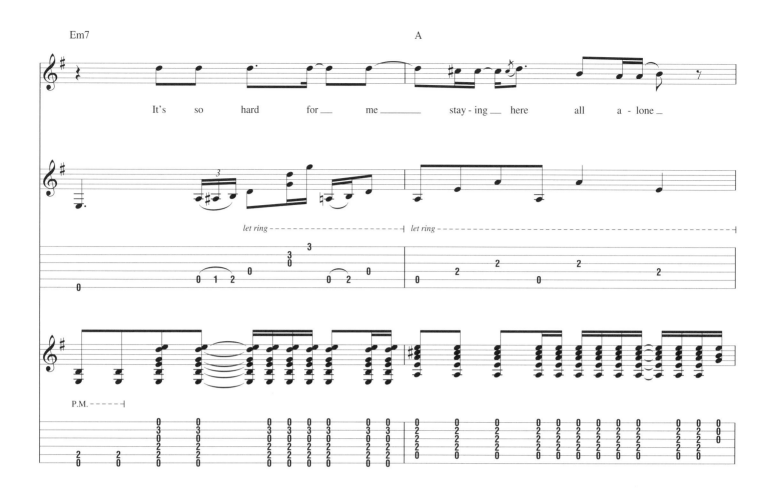

It's so hard for ___ me ___ stay-ing ___ here all a - lone ___

when you could be tak - ing me ___ for a ri - i -

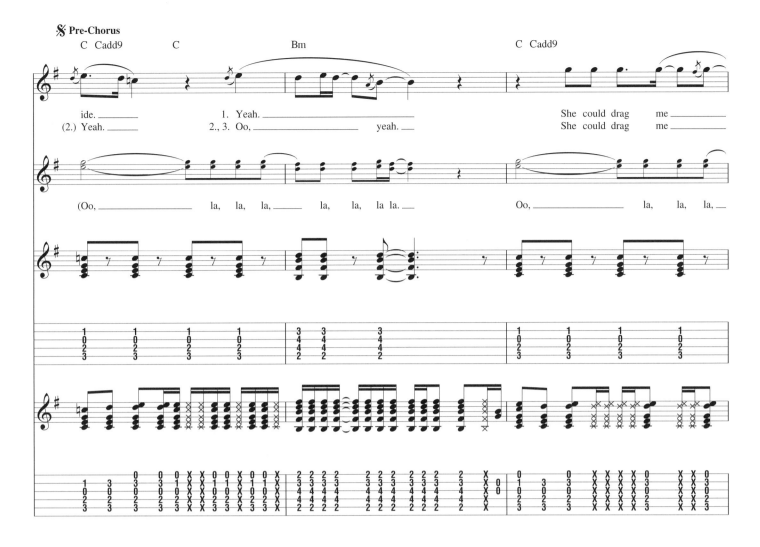

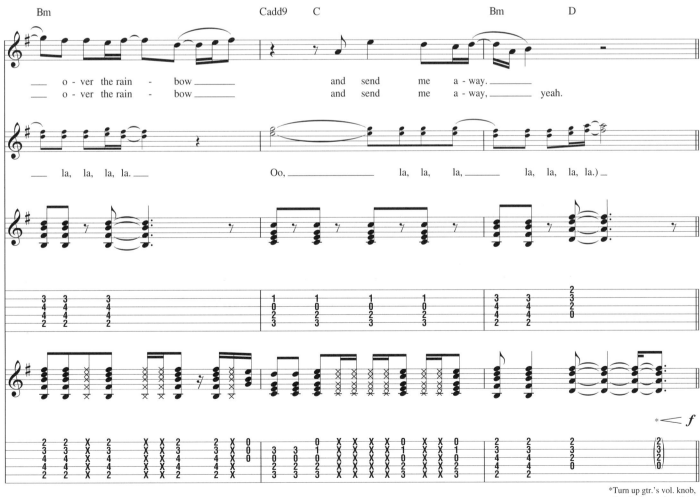

*Turn up gtr.'s vol. knob,
thereby increasing dist.

Chorus

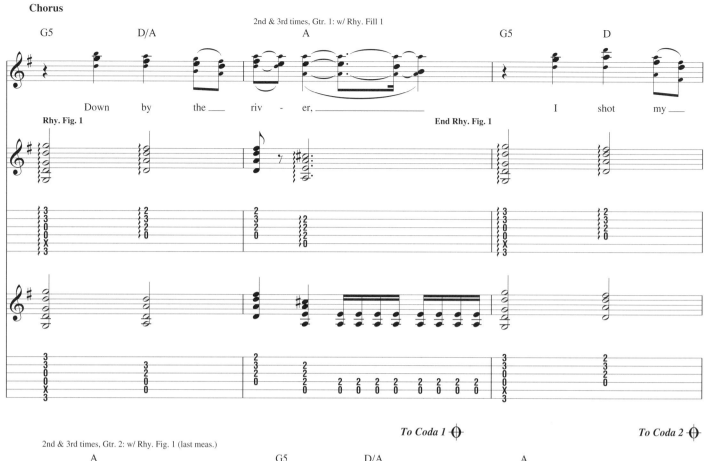

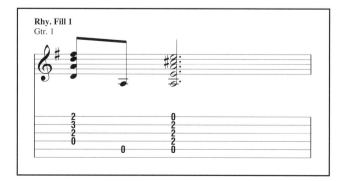

Interlude

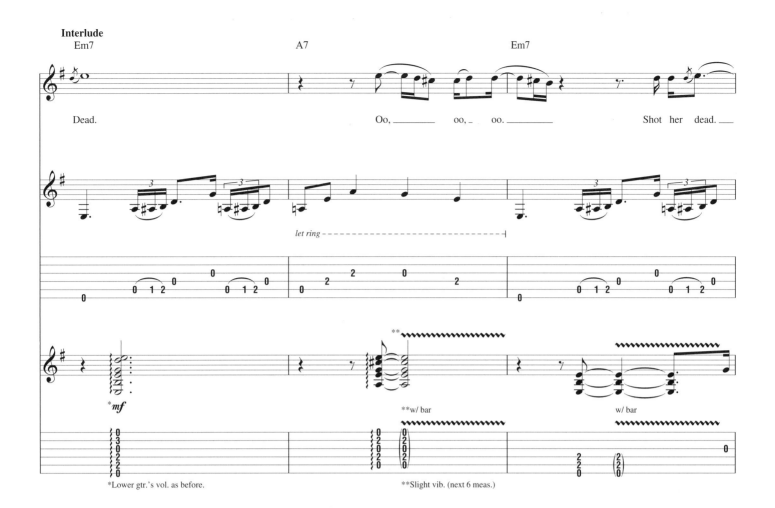

*Lower gtr.'s vol. as before.   **Slight vib. (next 6 meas.)

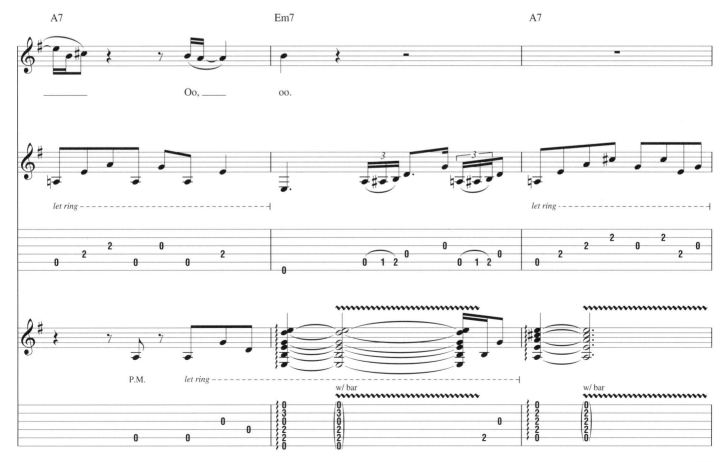

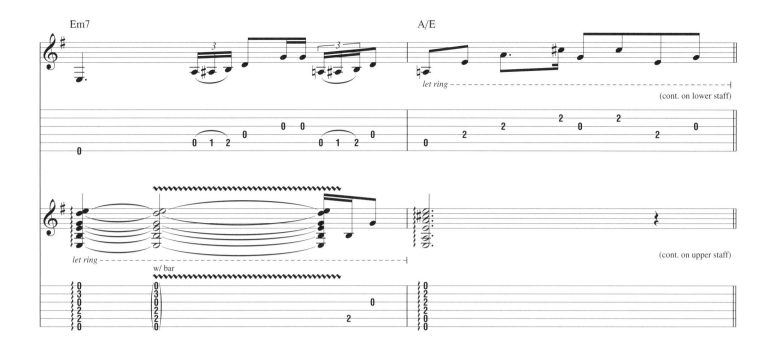

Guitar Solo

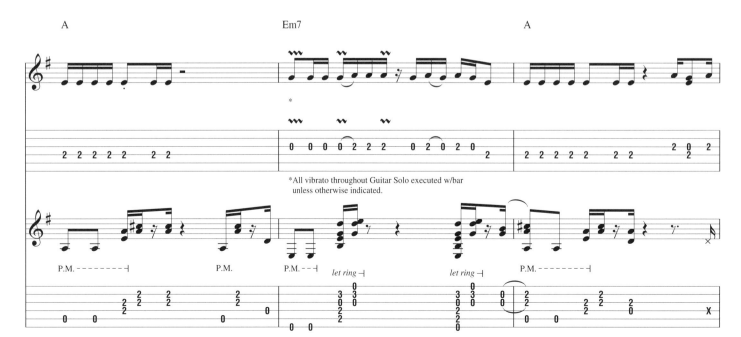

*All vibrato throughout Guitar Solo executed w/bar
unless otherwise indicated.

Em7   A   Em7

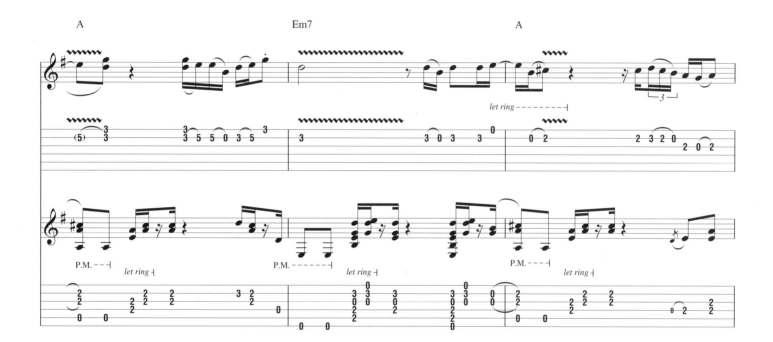

A   Em7   A

Em7   A   Em7

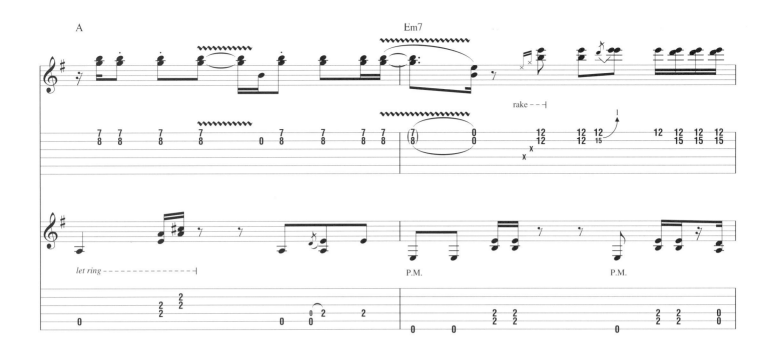

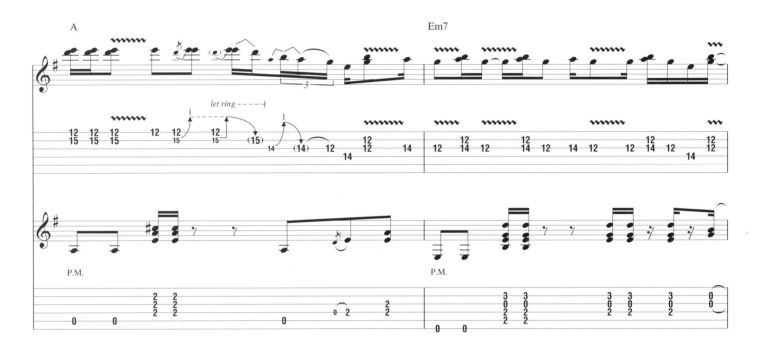

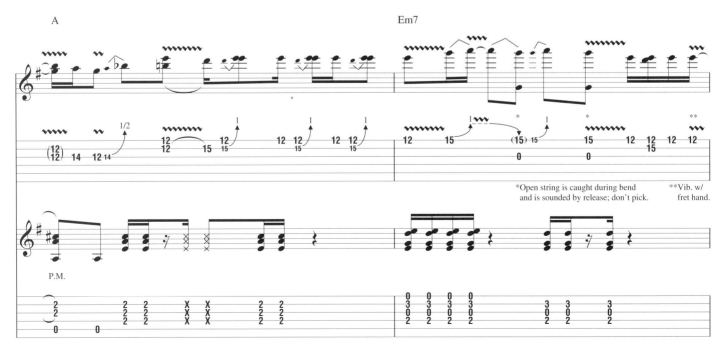

*Open string is caught during bend
and is sounded by release; don't pick.

**Vib. w/
fret hand.

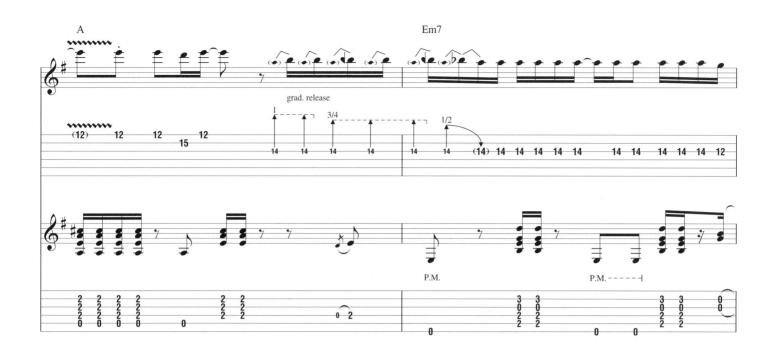

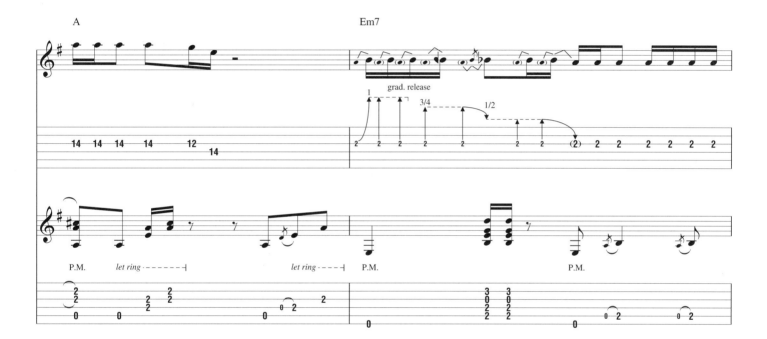

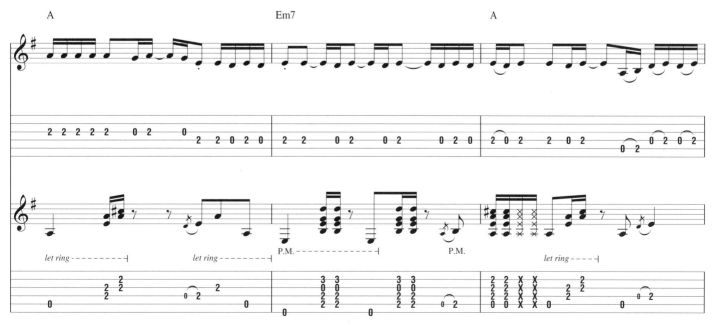

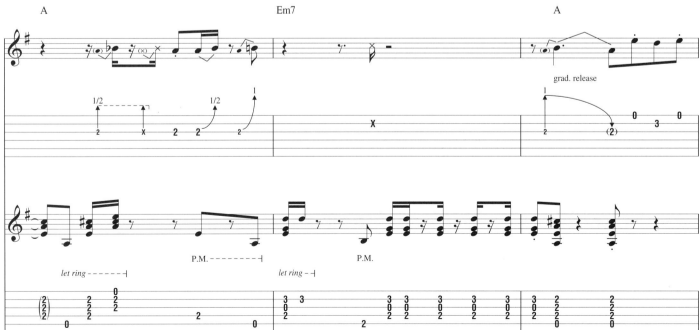

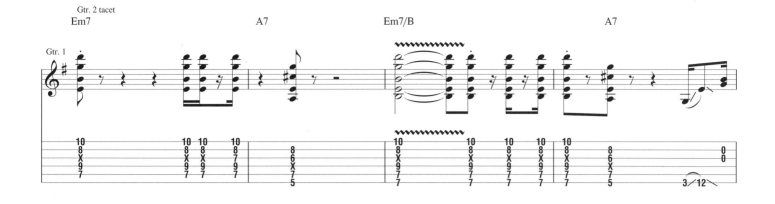

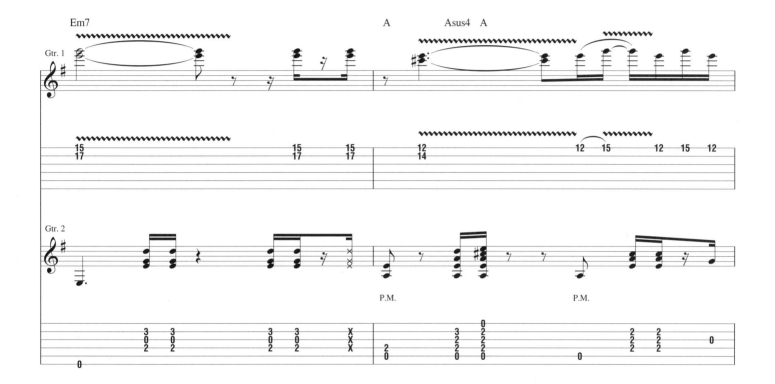

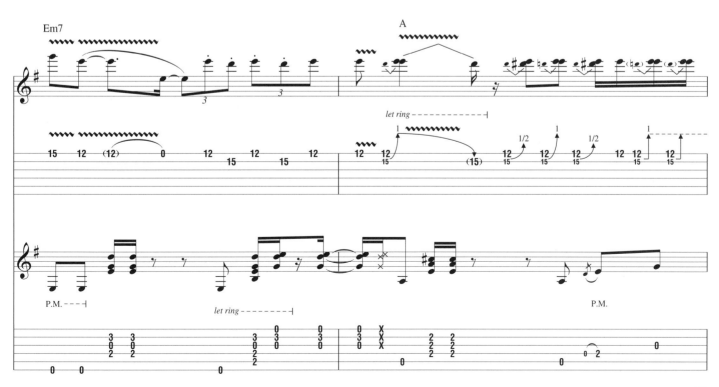

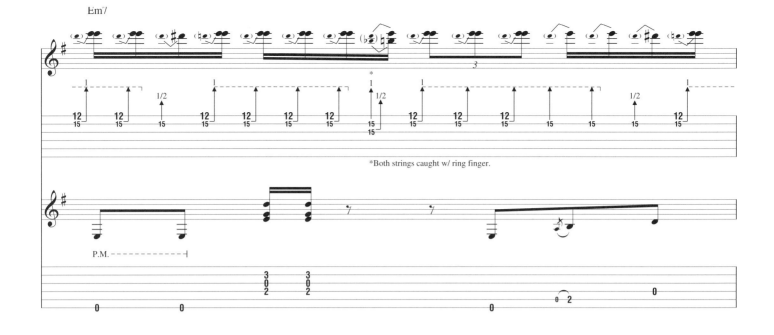

*Both strings caught w/ ring finger.

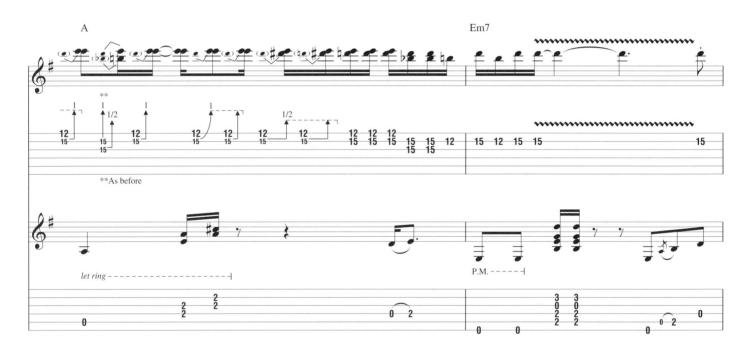

**As before

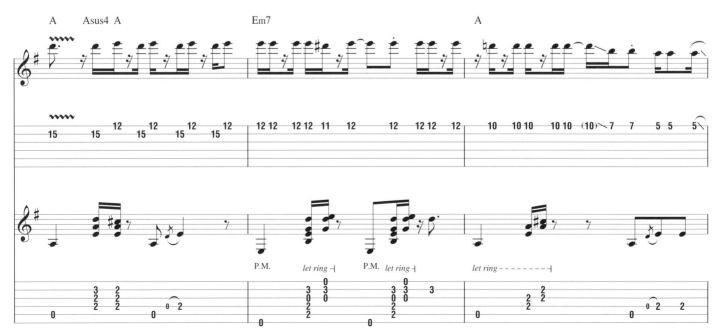

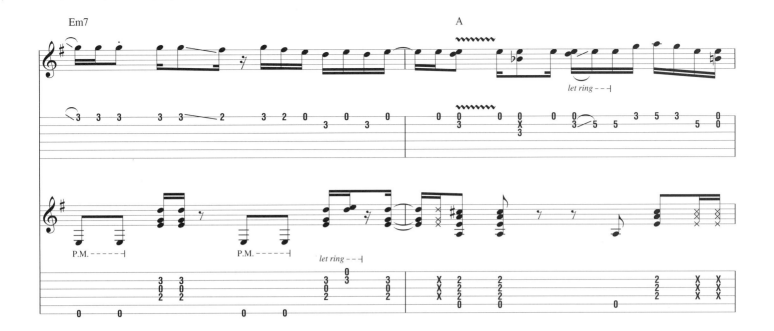

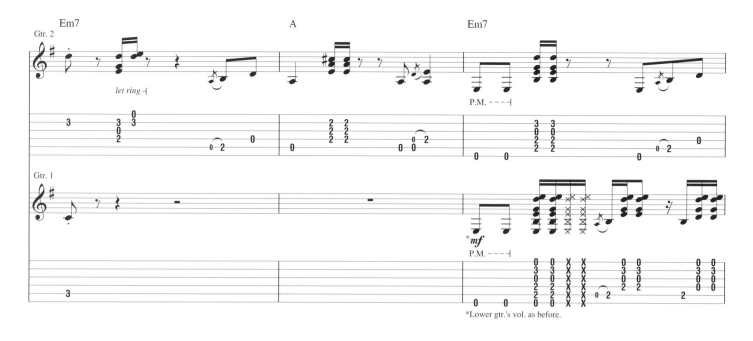

*Lower gtr.'s vol. as before.

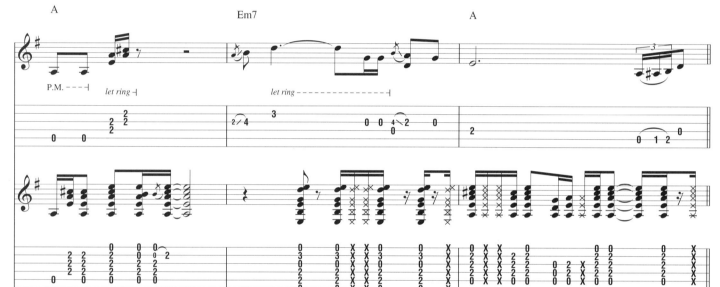

Verse

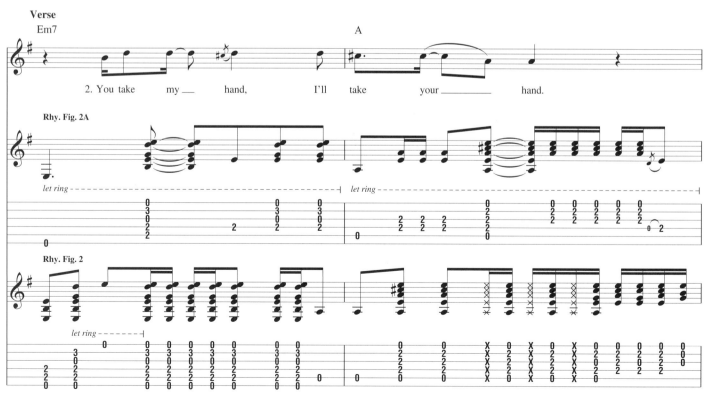

2. You take my ___ hand, I'll take your ___ hand.

To-geth-er _____ we may ___ get a - way. _____

This much mad - ness ___ is _____ too ___ much sor - row. ___

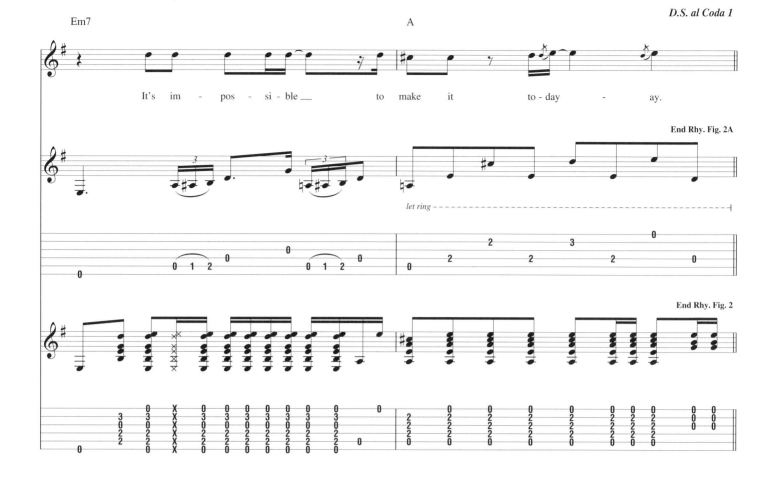

It's im - pos - si - ble ___ to make it to - day - ay.

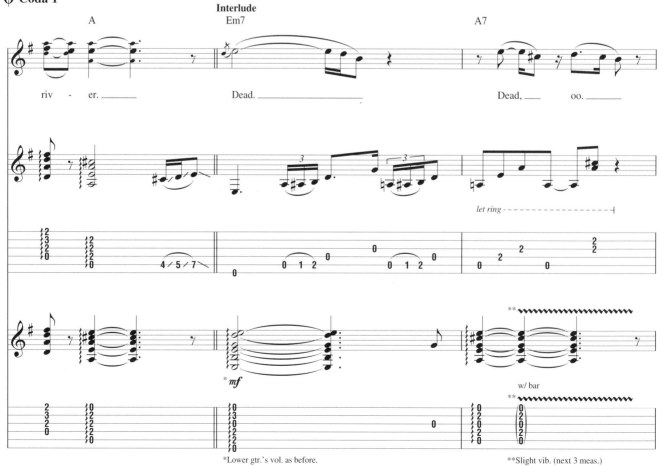

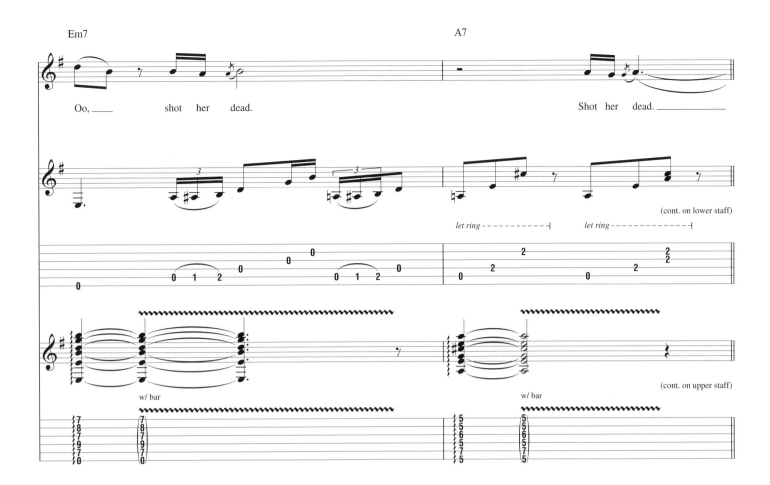

Oo, _____ shot her dead. Shot her dead. _____

(cont. on lower staff)

let ring - - - - - - - - -   let ring - - - - - - - - -

w/ bar   w/ bar

(cont. on upper staff)

Guitar Solo

let ring - - - - - - - - -

Gtr. 1

Gtr. 2

let ring - - - - -

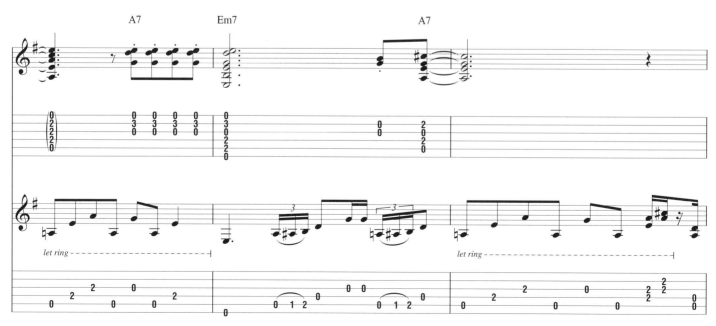

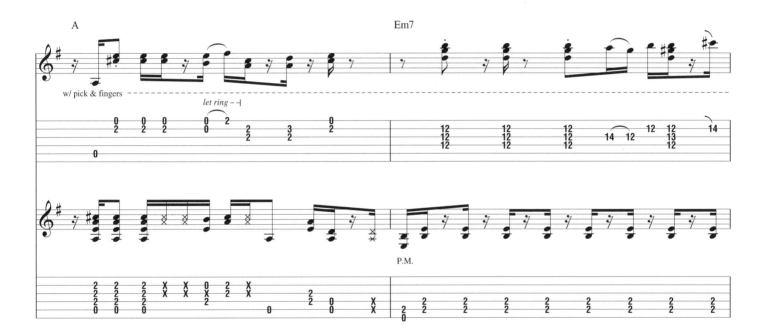

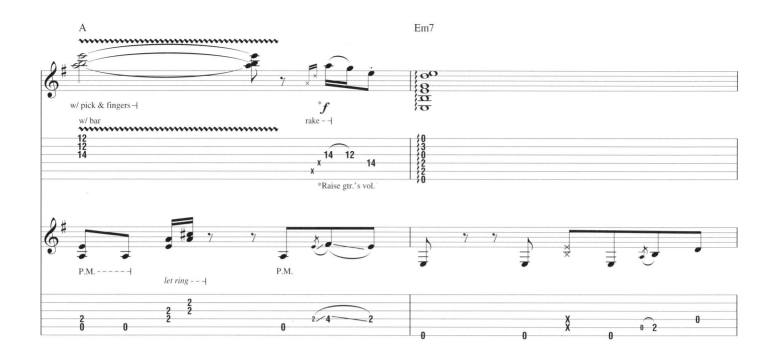

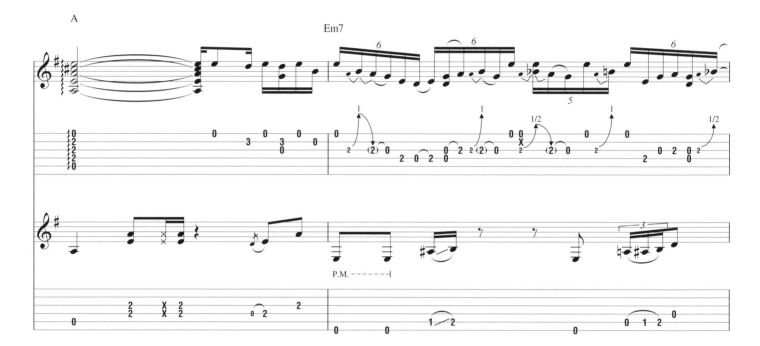

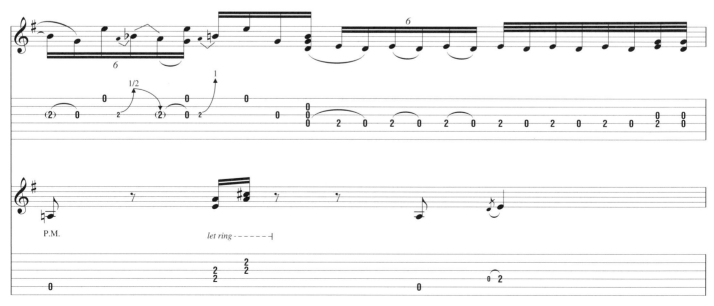

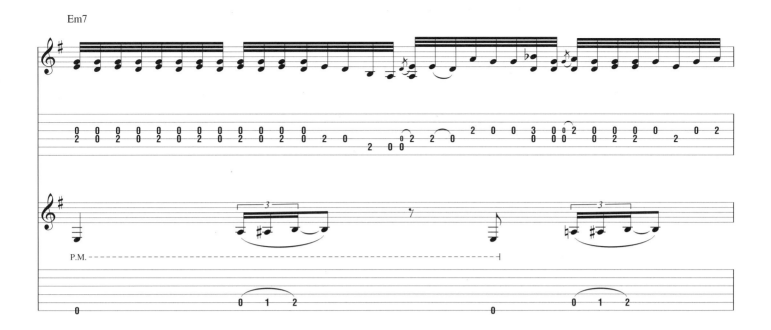

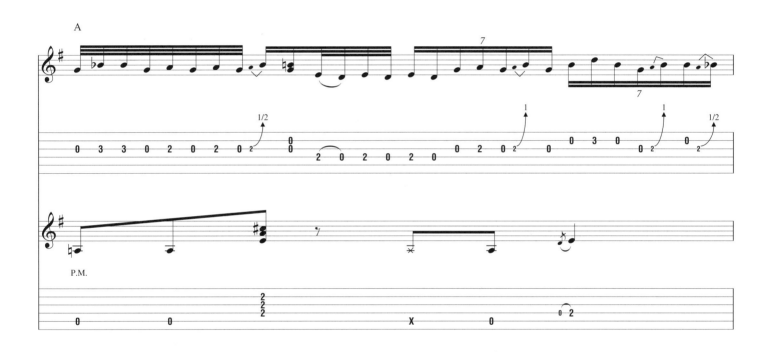

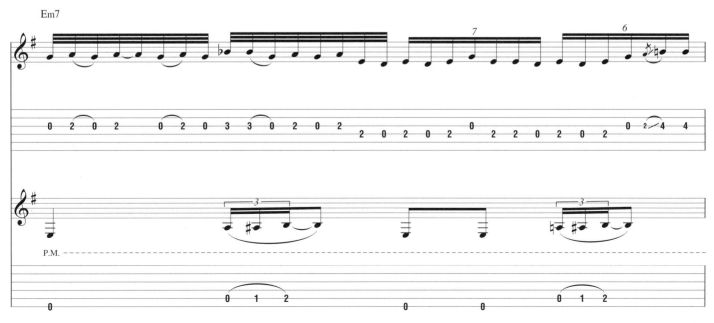

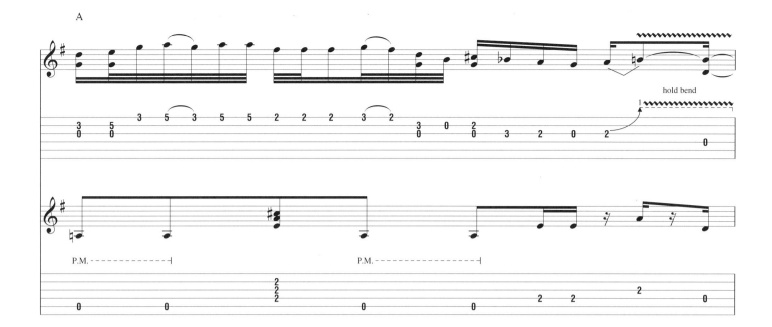

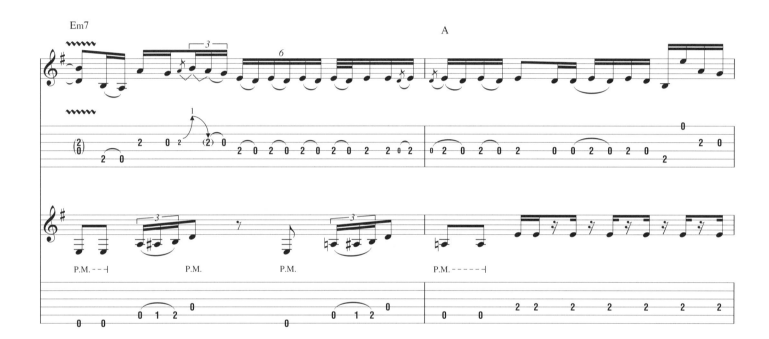

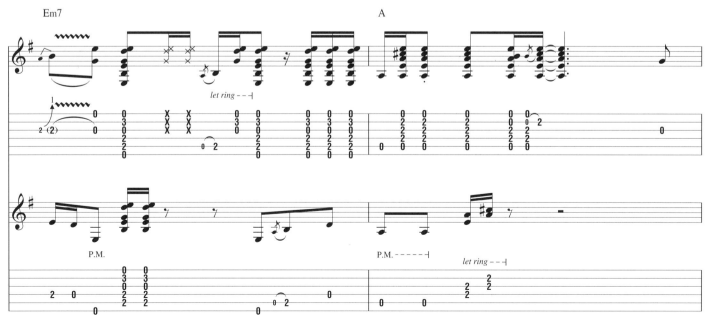

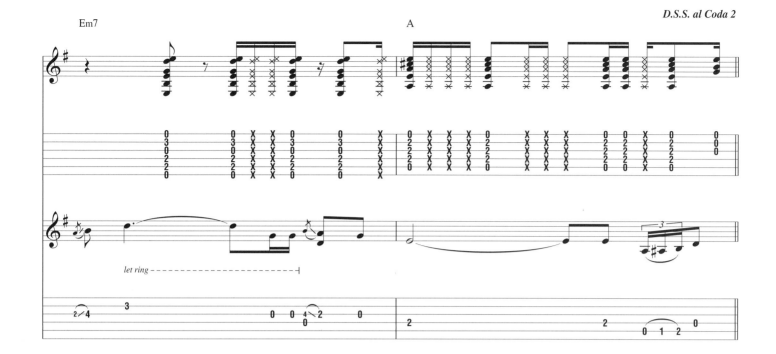

⊕ Coda 2

Gtr. 2: w/ Rhy. Fig. 1 (till fade)

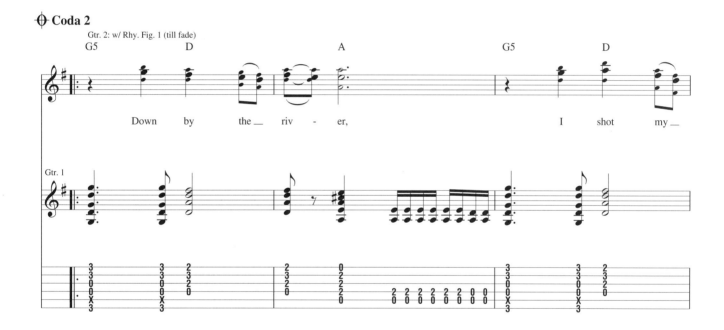

Down by the ___ riv - er, I shot my ___

Repeat and fade

ba - by. Down by the ___ riv - er.

THE LOSING END
(WHEN YOU'RE ON)

I WENT IN TO TOWN TO SEE YOU YESTERDAY
BUT YOU WERE NOT HOME
SO I TALKED TO SOME OLD FRIENDS FOR A WHILE
BEFORE I WANDERED OFF ALONE

IT'S SO HARD FOR ME NOW
BUT I'LL MAKE IT SOMEHOW
THOUGH I KNOW I'LL NEVER BE THE SAME
WON'T YOU EVER CHANGE YOUR WAYS
IT'S SO HARD TO MAKE LOVE PAY
WHEN YOU'RE ON THE LOSING END
AND I FEEL THAT WAY AGAIN

WELL, I MISS YOU MORE THAN EVER
SINCE YOU'RE GONE I CAN HARDLY MAINTAIN
THINGS ARE DIFFERENT 'ROUND HERE EVERY NIGHT
MY TEARS FALL DOWN LIKE RAIN

IT'S SO HARD FOR ME NOW
BUT I'LL MAKE IT SOMEHOW
THOUGH I KNOW I'LL NEVER BE THE SAME
WON'T YOU EVER CHANGE YOUR WAYS
IT'S SO HARD TO MAKE LOVE PAY
WHEN YOU'RE ON THE LOSING END
AND I FEEL THAT WAY AGAIN

The Losing End
(When You're On)

Words and Music by Neil Young

Chorus

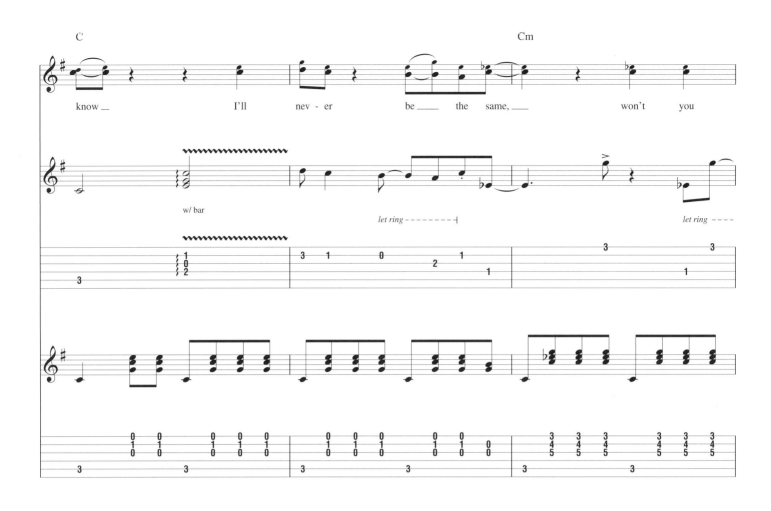

know ___   I'll   nev - er   be ___ the   same, ___   won't   you

ev - er   change ___ your   ways? ___   It's   so   hard ___ to   make   love

pay, — when you're on ___ the los - ing end. ___

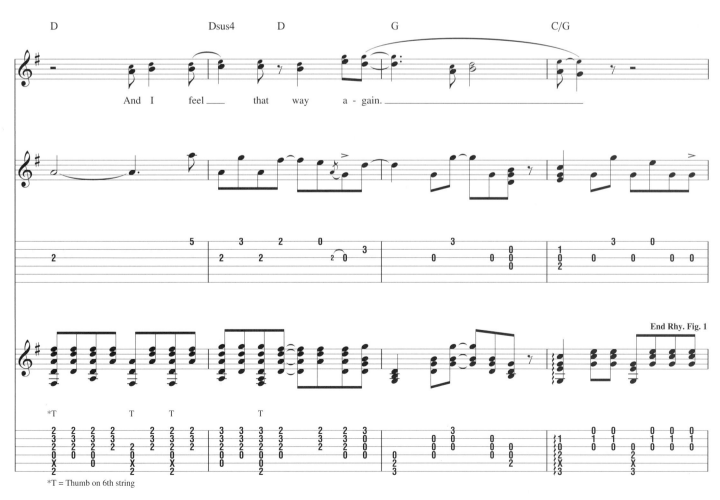

And I feel ___ that way a - gain.

End Rhy. Fig. 1

*T = Thumb on 6th string

2. Well, I miss ___

(cont. in slashes)

Verse

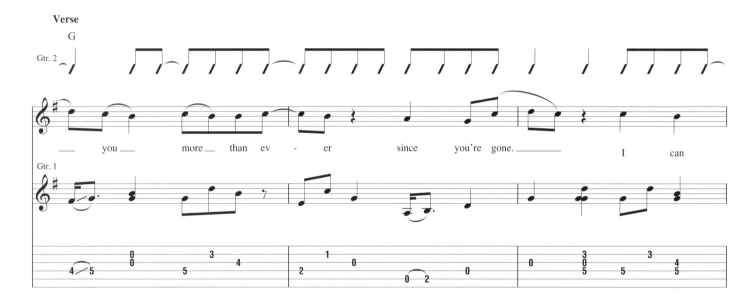

___ you ___ more ___ than ev - er since you're gone. _____ I can

hard - ly main - tain. _____

let ring -------------------

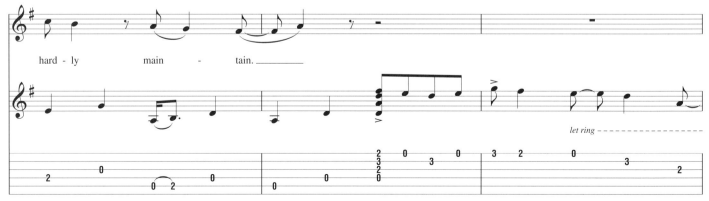

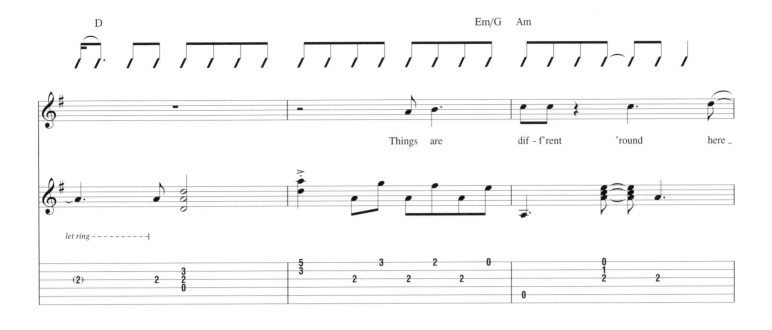

Things are   dif - f'rent   'round   here

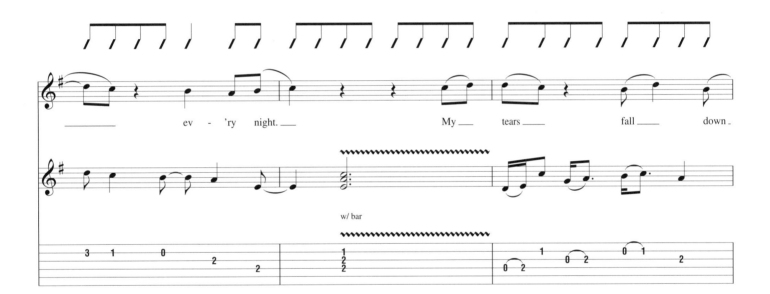

_____   ev - 'ry   night. _____   My ___   tears ___   fall ___   down ___

w/ bar

___   like   rain. _____   It's   so

Chorus

Gtr. 2: w/ Rhy. Fig. 1

hard ___ for me now, _____ but I'll make ___ it ___ some -

how. __ Though I ___ know _ I'll nev - er be __ the same, ___ won't you

ev - er change _ your ways? __ It's so hard to make love pay, __ when you're on __

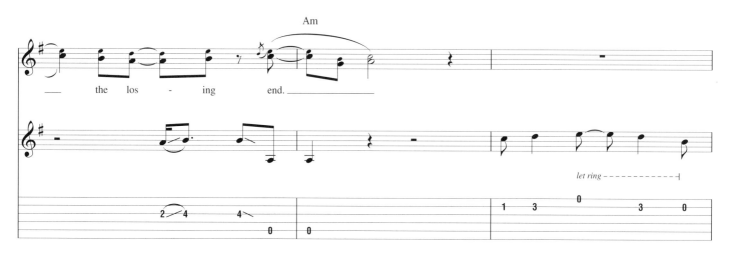

__ the los - ing end. _____

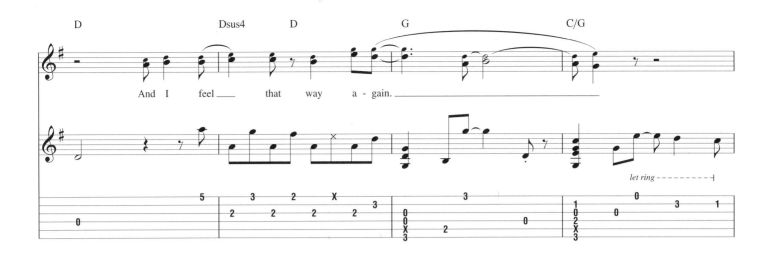

And I feel ___ that way a - gain. ___

Guitar Solo

Spoken: Alright, Wilson ... pick it!

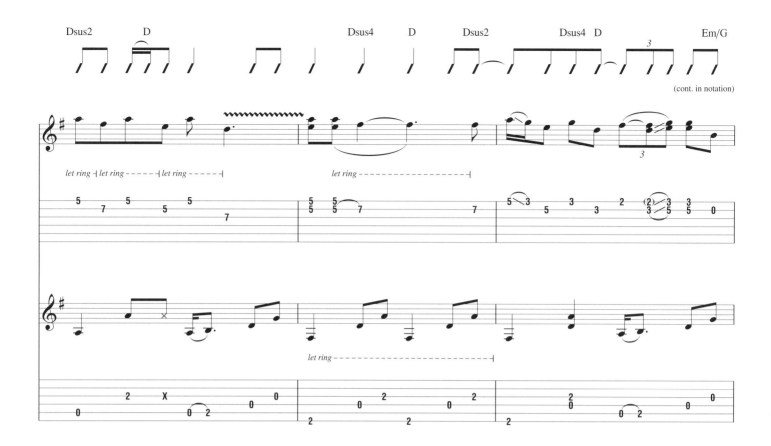

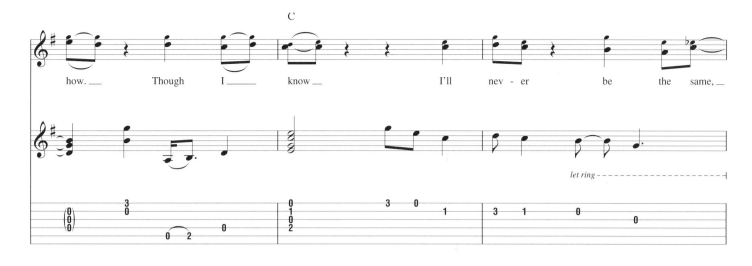

how. ___ Though I ___ know ___ I'll nev - er be the same, ___

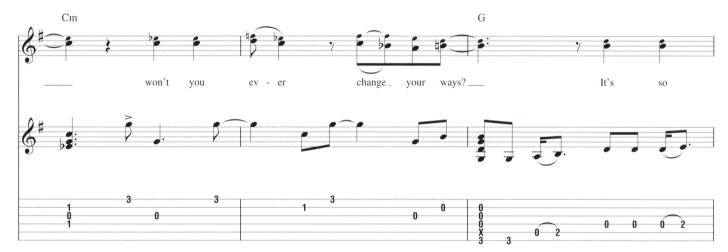

___ won't you ev - er change ___ your ways? ___ It's so

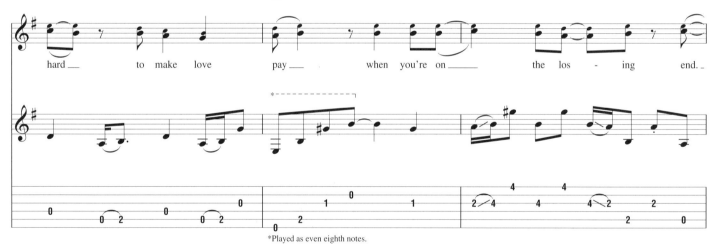

hard ___ to make love pay ___ when you're on ___ the los - ing end. ___

*Played as even eighth notes.

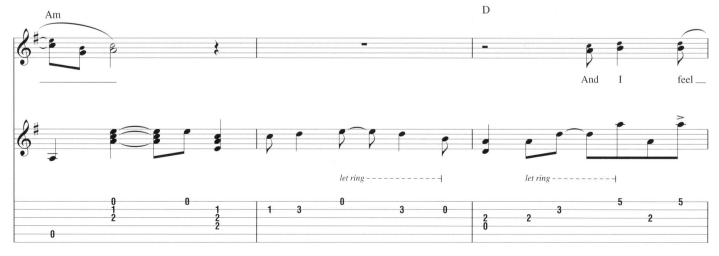

And I feel ___

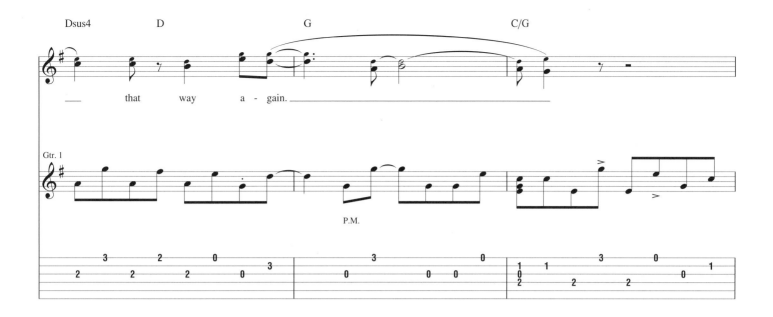

that way a - gain.

RUNNING DRY
(REQUIEM FOR THE ROCKETS)

OH PLEASE HELP ME, OH PLEASE HELP ME
I'M LIVING BY MYSELF
I NEED SOMEONE TO COMFORT ME
I NEED SOMEONE TO TELL

I'M SORRY FOR THE THINGS I'VE DONE
I'VE SHAMED MYSELF WITH LIES
SOON THESE THINGS ARE OVERCOME
AND CAN'T BE RECOGNIZED

I LEFT MY LOVE
WITH RIBBONS ON
AND WATER IN HER EYES
I TOOK FROM HER THE LOVE I'VE WON
AND TURNED IT TO THE SKY

I'M SORRY FOR THE THINGS I'VE DONE
I'VE CHAINED MYSELF WITH LIES
MY CRUELTY HAS PUNCTURED ME
AND NOW I'M RUNNING DRY

I'M SORRY FOR THE THINGS I'VE DONE
I'VE SHAMED MYSELF WITH LIES
BUT SOON THESE THINGS ARE OVERCOME
AND CAN'T BE RECOGNIZED

Running Dry
(Requiem for the Rockets)

Words and Music by Neil Young

Drop D tuning:
(low to high) D-A-D-G-B-E

*Chord symbols reflect basic harmony.

Verse

please help me. ___ Oh, please ___ help me; I'm liv - ing by my - self. I

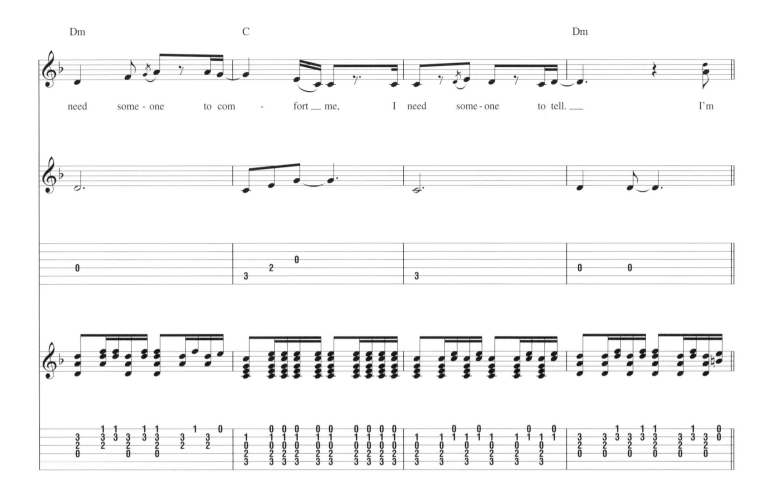

need some-one to com - fort __ me, I need some-one to tell. __ I'm

Chorus

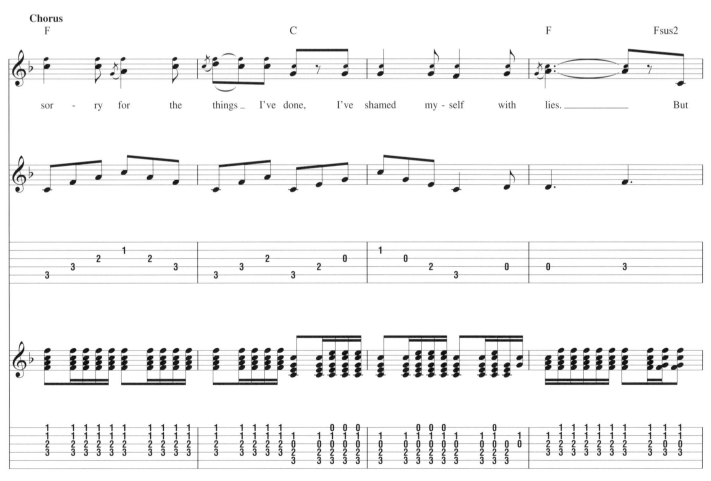

sor - ry for the things __ I've done, I've shamed my-self with lies. _____ But

83

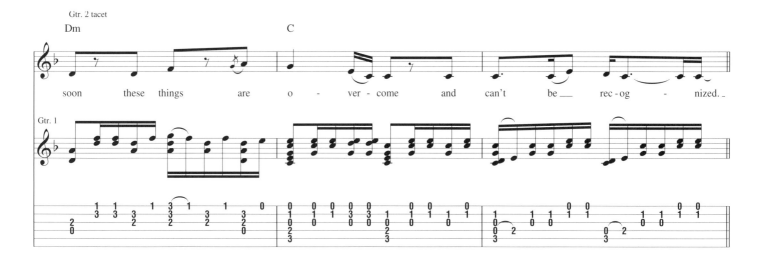

soon these things are o - ver - come and can't be __ rec - og - nized. __

Verse

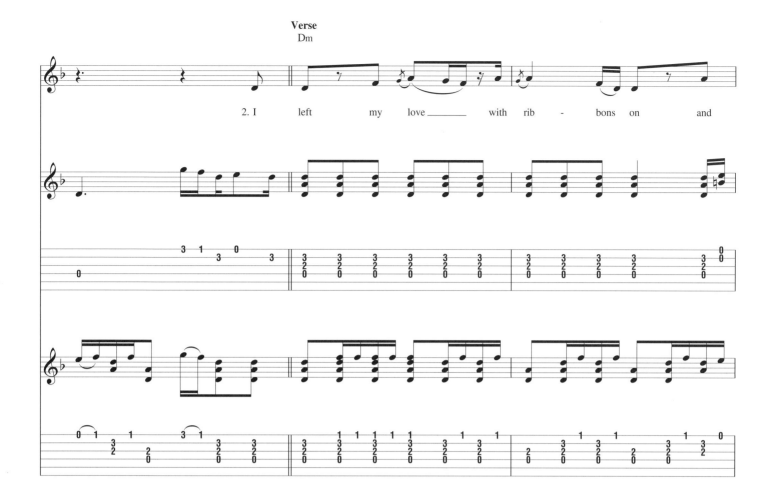

2. I left my love _____ with rib - bons on and

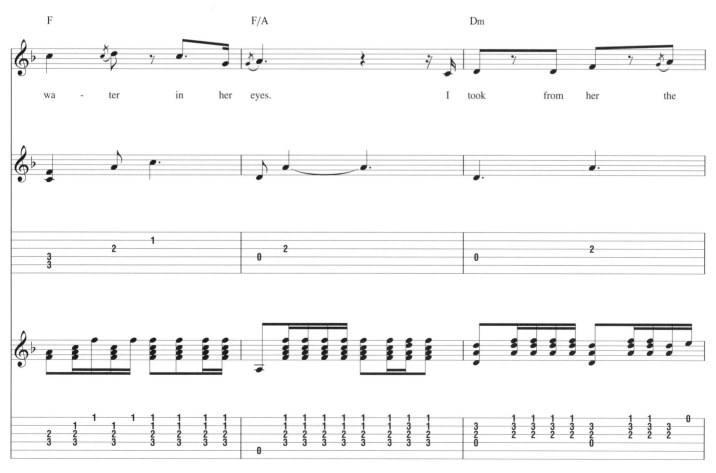

wa - ter in her eyes. I took from her the

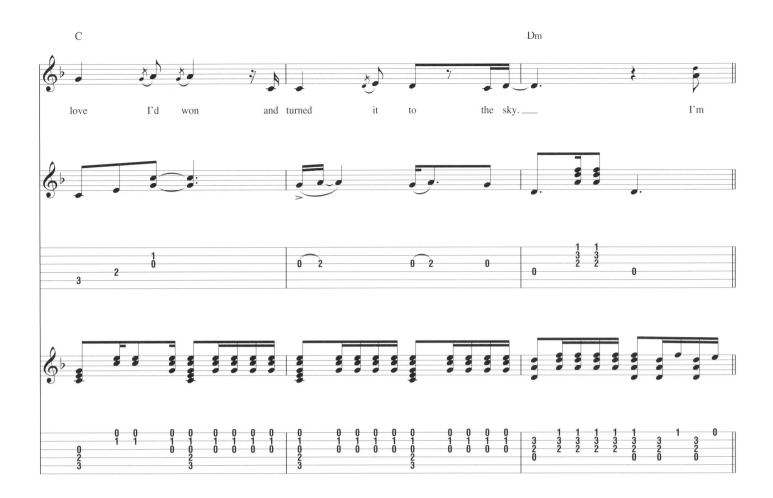

love   I'd   won   and   turned   it   to   the   sky. __   I'm

Chorus

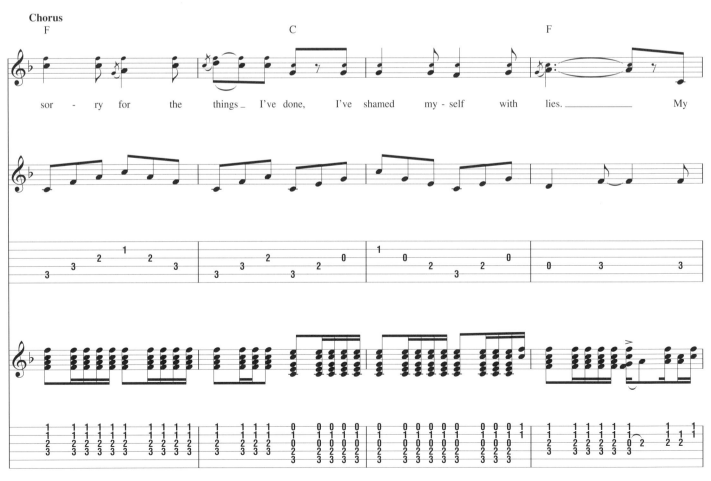

sor - ry   for   the   things _   I've   done,   I've   shamed   my - self   with   lies. _____   My

cru - el - ty has punc - tured _ me, and now I'm run - ning dry.

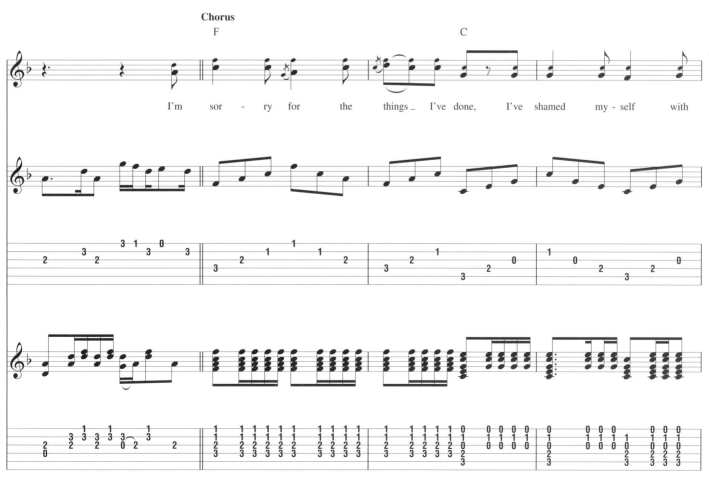

Chorus

I'm sor - ry for the things _ I've done, I've shamed my - self with

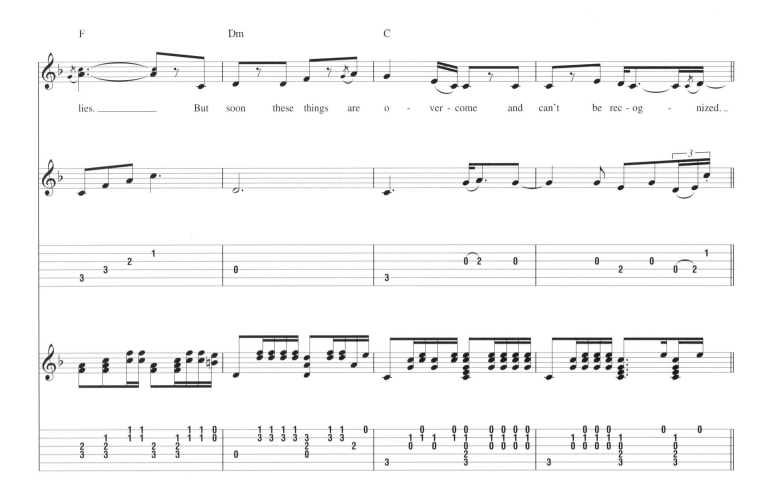

lies. _____ But soon these things are o - ver - come and can't be rec - og - nized. _

Interlude

Dm

Chorus

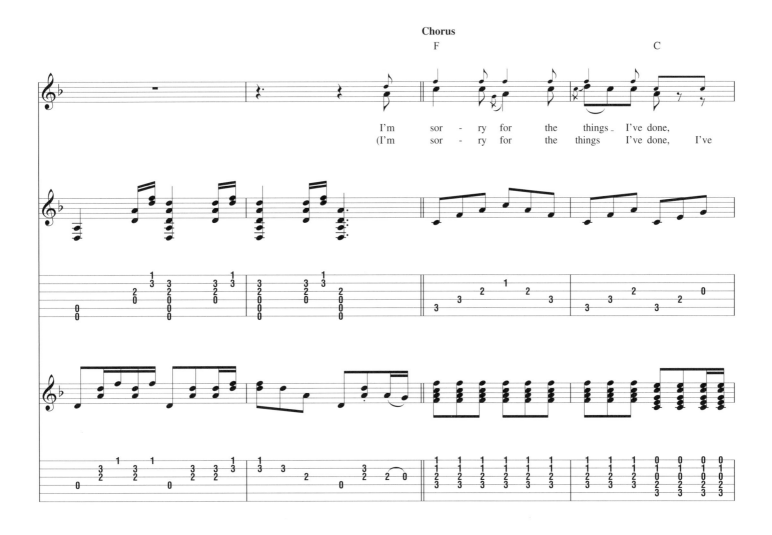

I'm   sor - ry for   the   things __ I've done,
(I'm   sor - ry for   the   things   I've done,   I've

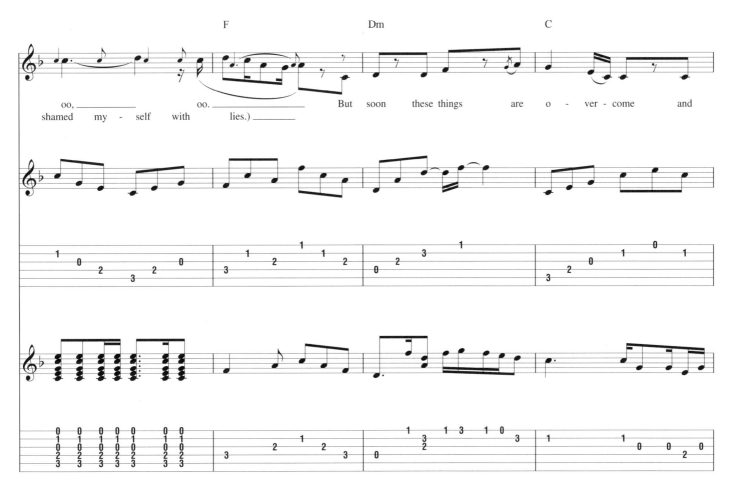

oo, _____   oo. _____   But soon   these things   are o - ver - come   and
shamed   my - self   with   lies.) _____

Outro

Begin fade

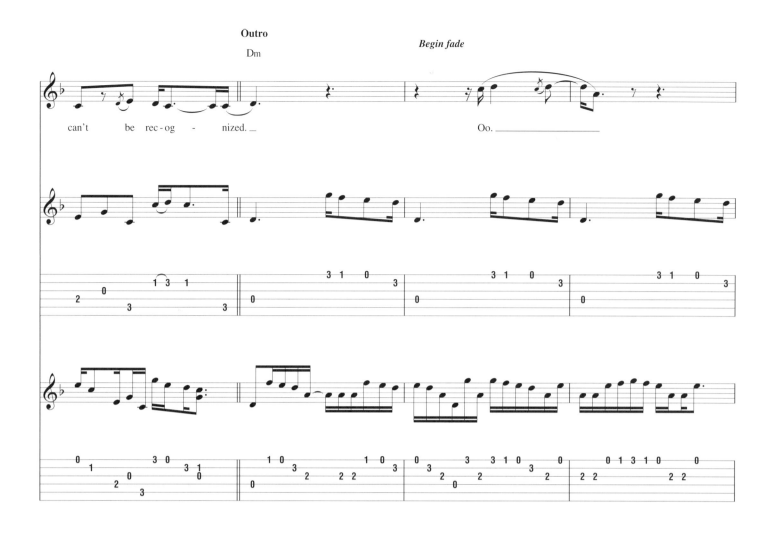

can't be rec-og - nized. ___ Oo. _____

Fade out

Oo. _____ Oo, _____ oo. _____

COWGIRL IN THE SAND

HELLO, COWGIRL IN THE SAND
IS THIS PLACE AT YOUR COMMAND?
CAN I STAY HERE FOR A WHILE?
CAN I SEE YOUR SWEET, SWEET SMILE?

OLD ENOUGH NOW TO CHANGE YOUR NAME
WHEN SO MANY LOVE YOU, IS IT THE SAME?
IT'S THE WOMAN IN YOU THAT MAKES YOU WANT TO PLAY THIS GAME

HELLO, RUBY IN THE DUST
HAS YOUR BAND BEGUN TO RUST?
AFTER ALL THE SIN WE'VE HAD
I WAS HOPING THAT WE'D TURN BAD

OLD ENOUGH TO CHANGE YOUR NAME
WHEN SO MANY LOVE YOU, IS IT THE SAME?
IT'S THE WOMAN IN YOU THAT MAKES YOU WANT TO PLAY THIS GAME

HELLO, WOMAN OF MY DREAMS
IS THIS NOT THE WAY IT SEEMS?
PURPLE WORDS ON A GRAY BACKGROUND
TO BE A WOMAN AND TO BE TURNED DOWN

OLD ENOUGH NOW TO CHANGE YOUR NAME
WHEN SO MANY LOVE YOU, IS IT THE SAME?
IT'S THE WOMAN IN YOU THAT MAKES YOU WANT TO PLAY THIS GAME

Cowgirl in the Sand

Words and Music by Neil Young

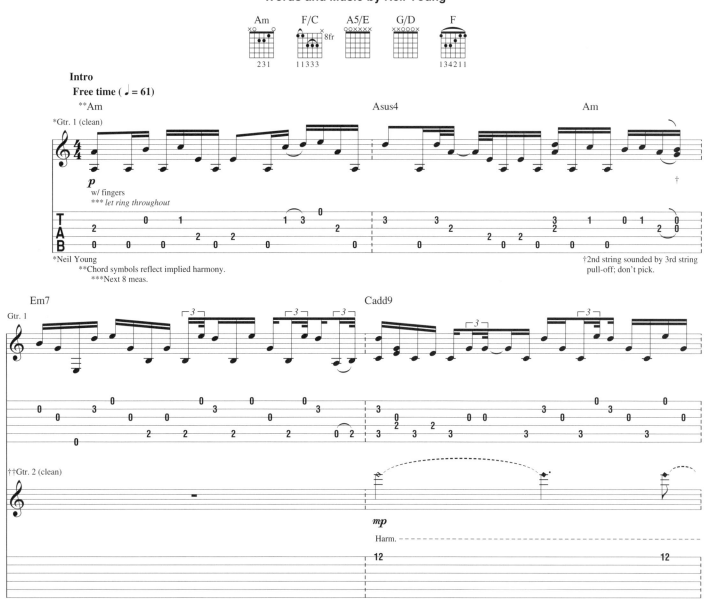

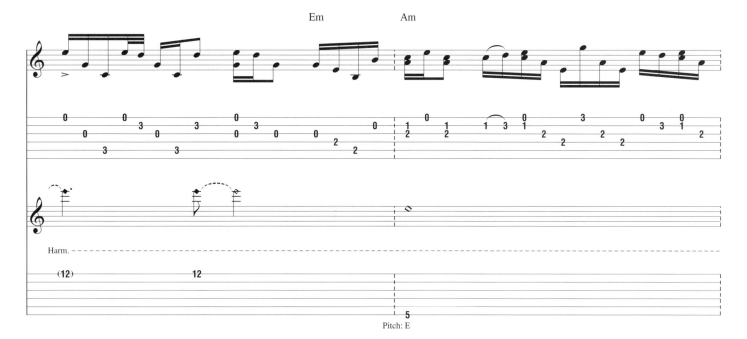

Asus2

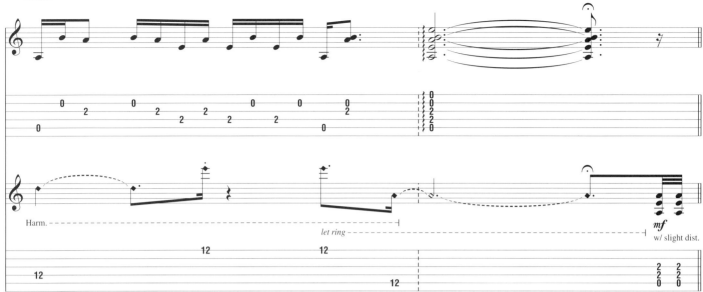

Interlude
Faster ♩ = 84

*Am   F   Am

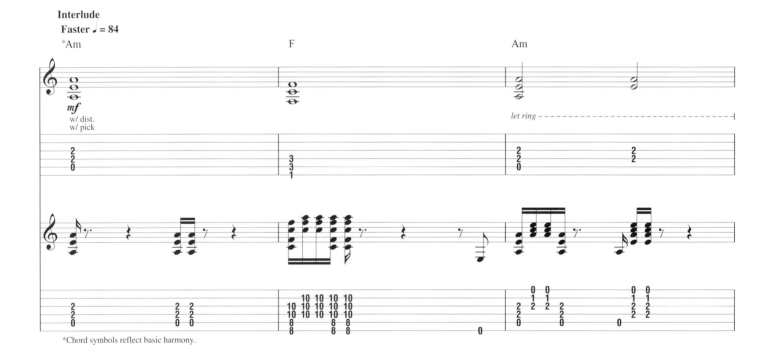

*Chord symbols reflect basic harmony.

Guitar Solo

F   Am

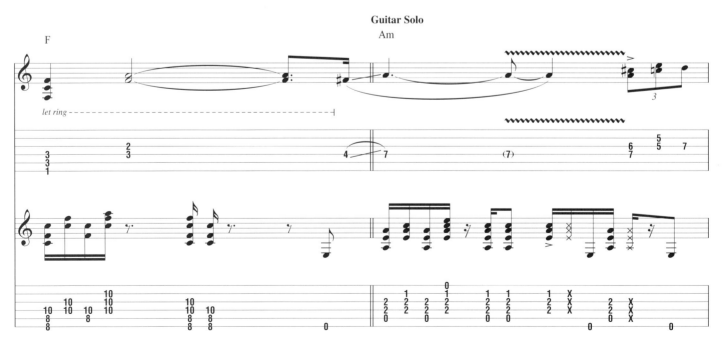

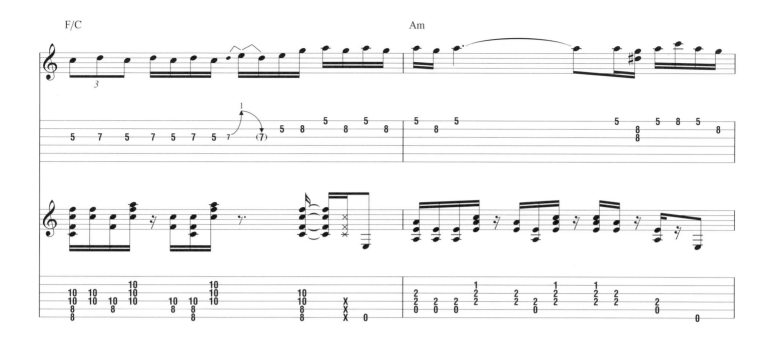

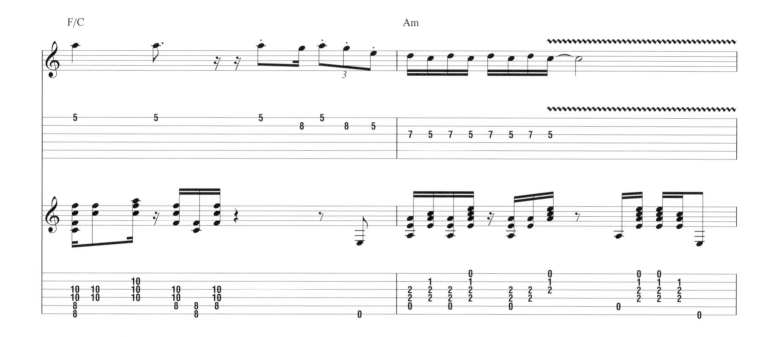

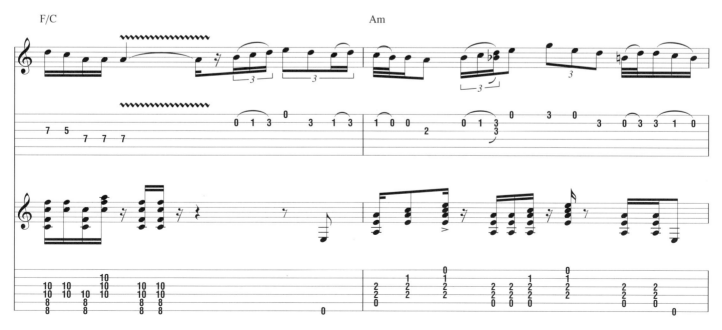

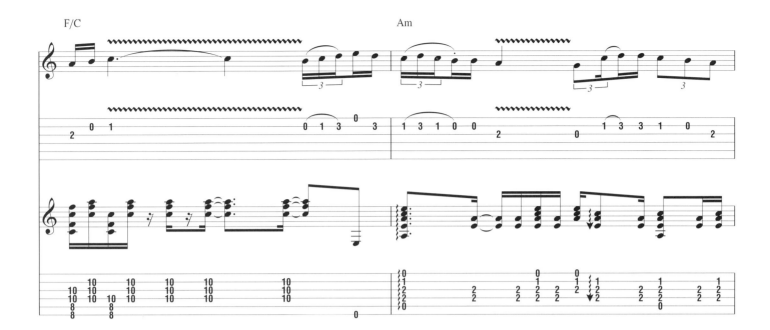

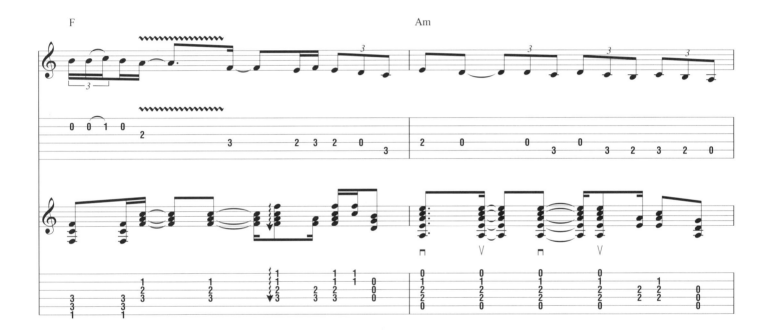

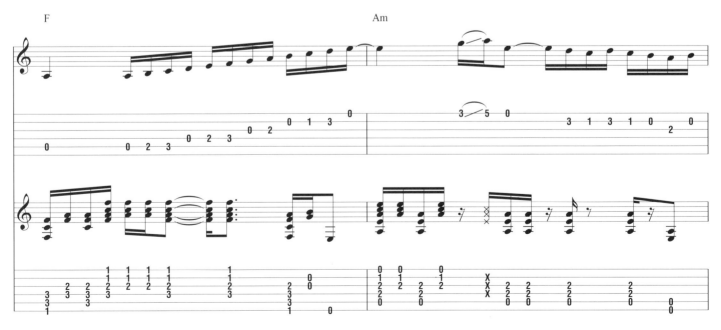

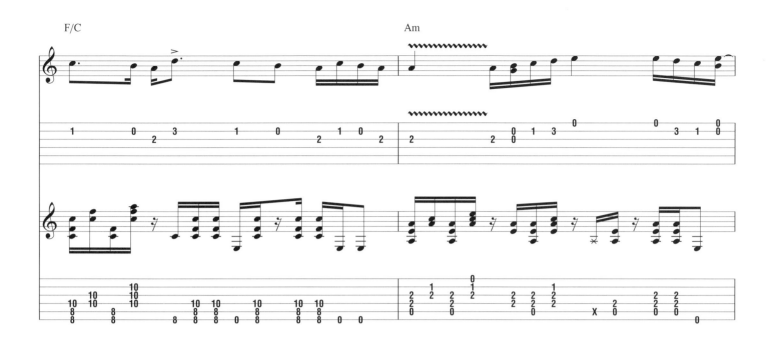

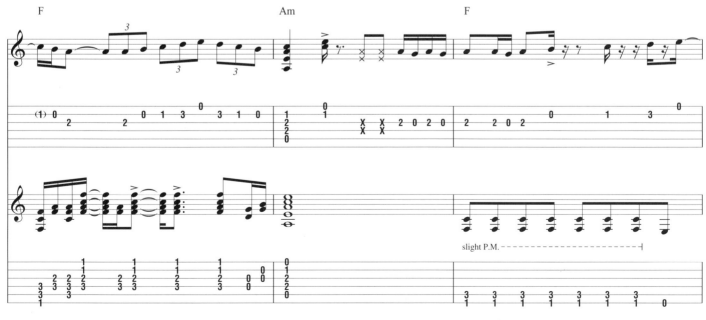

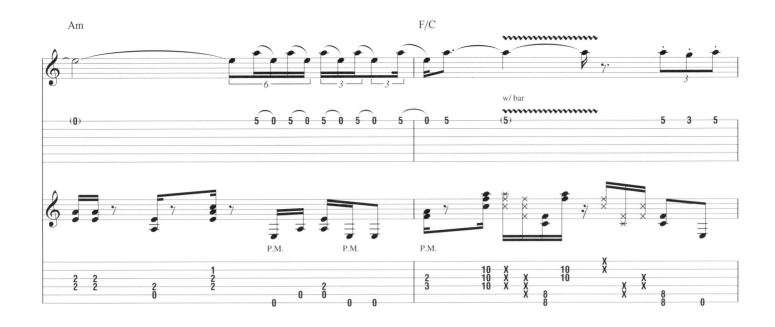

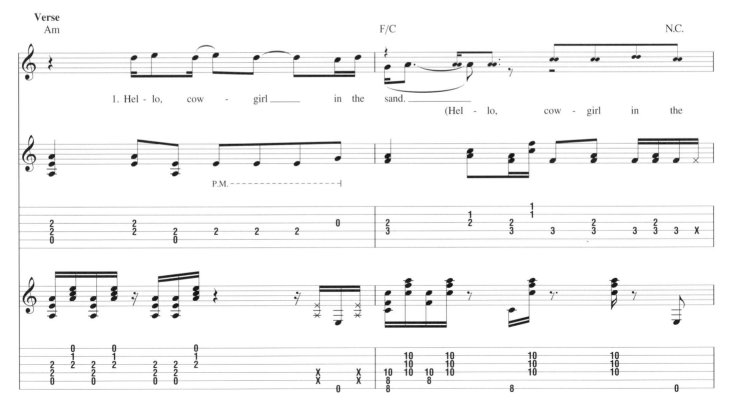

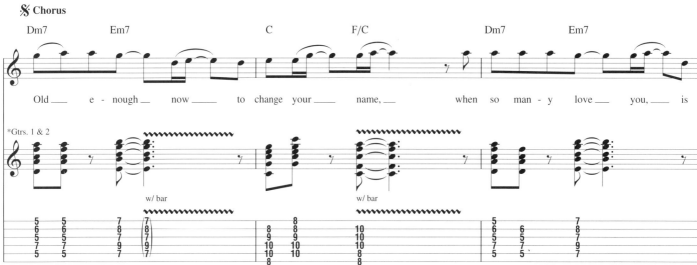

*Composite arrangement

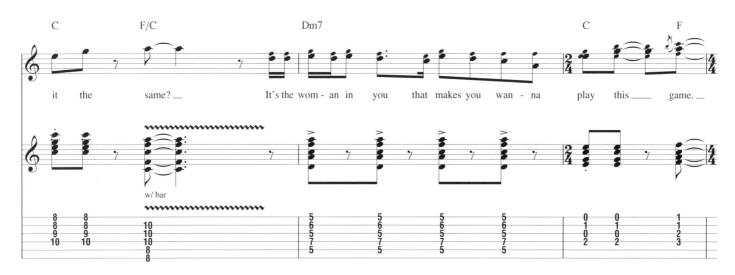

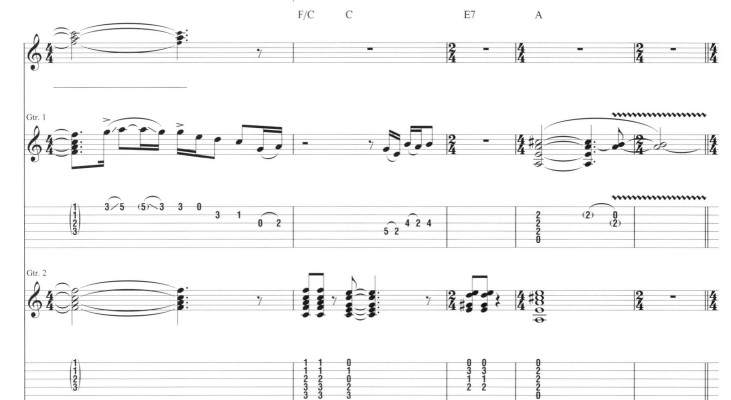

Interlude

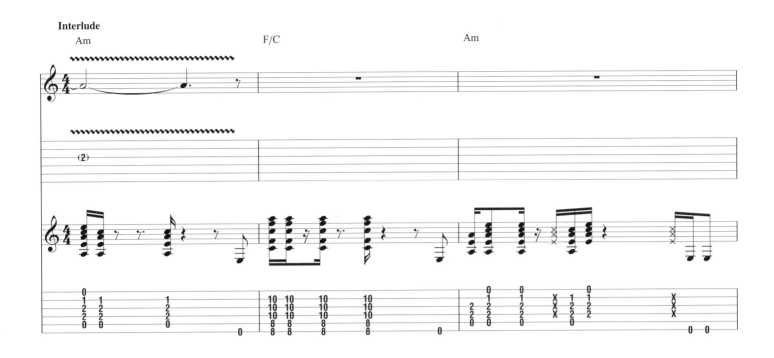

Guitar Solo

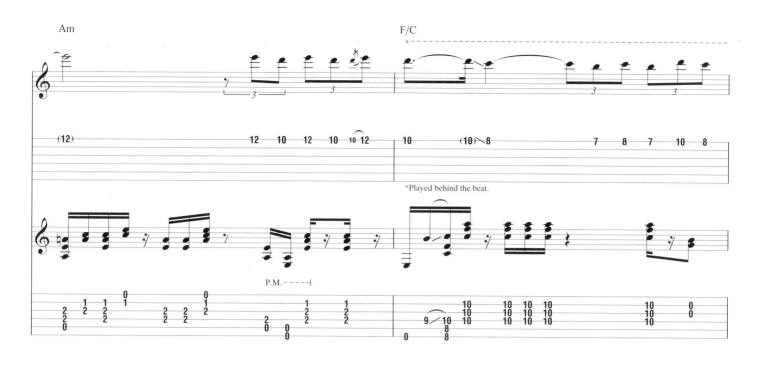

*Played behind the beat.

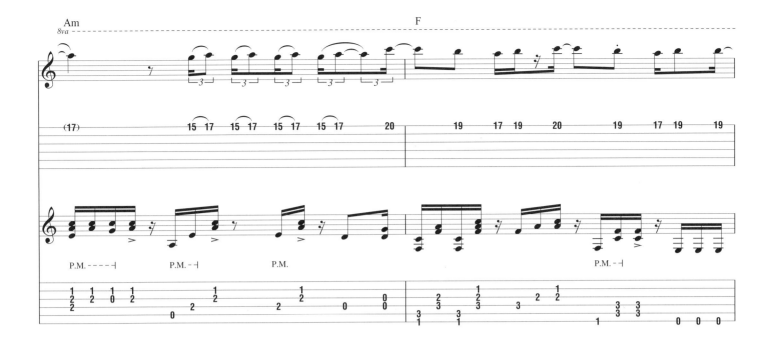

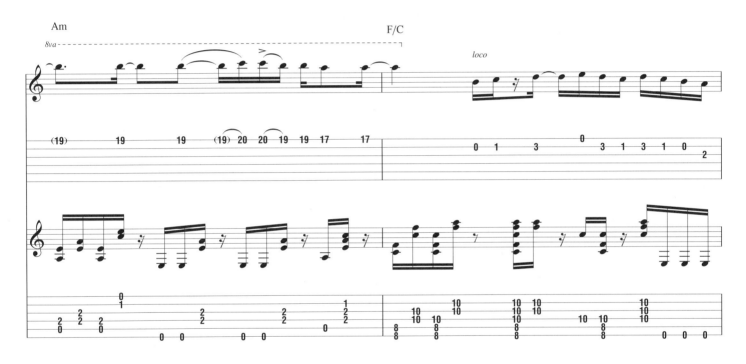

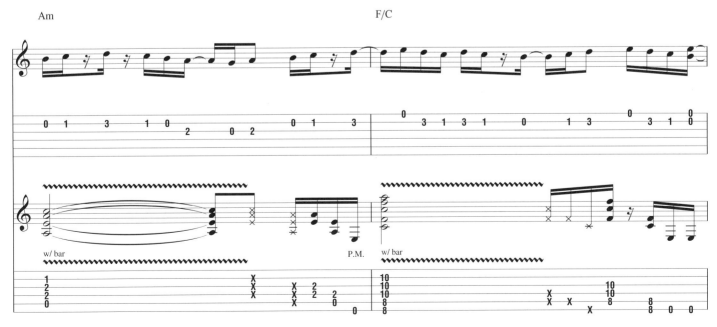

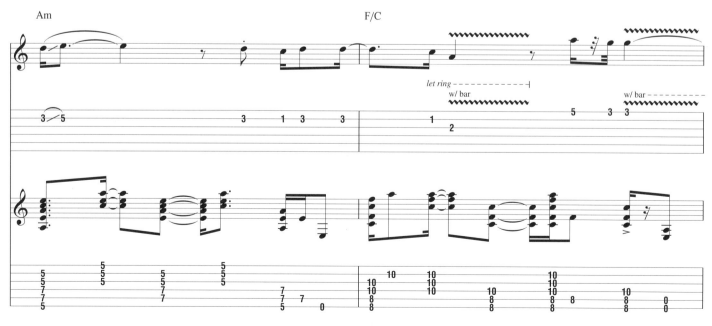

108

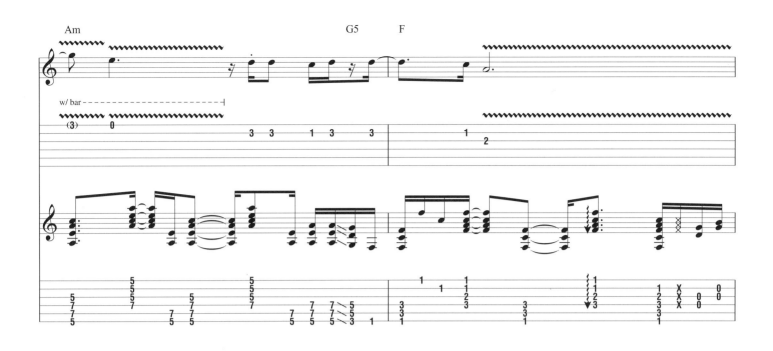

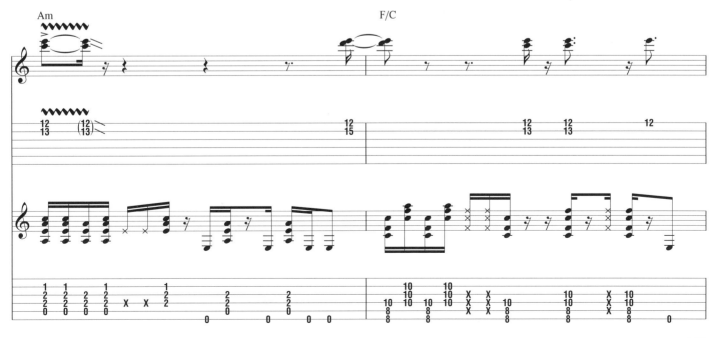

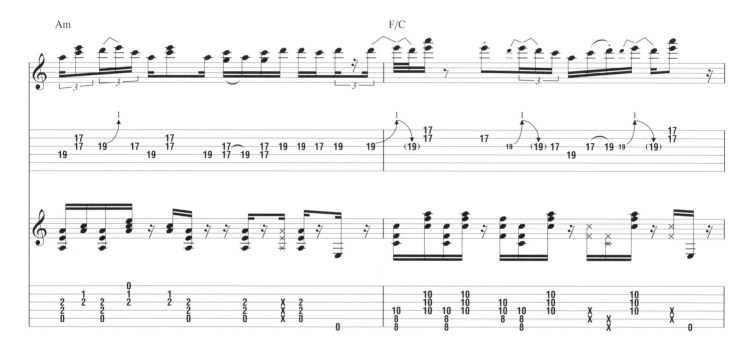

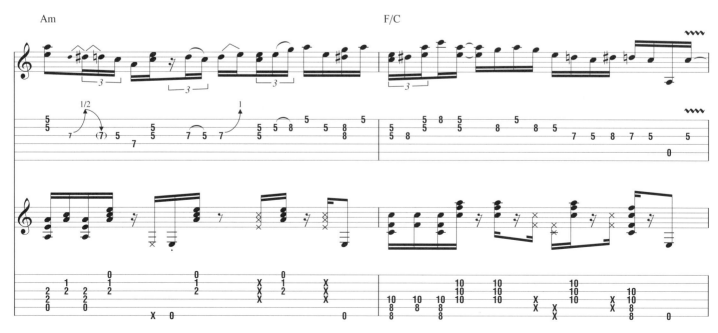

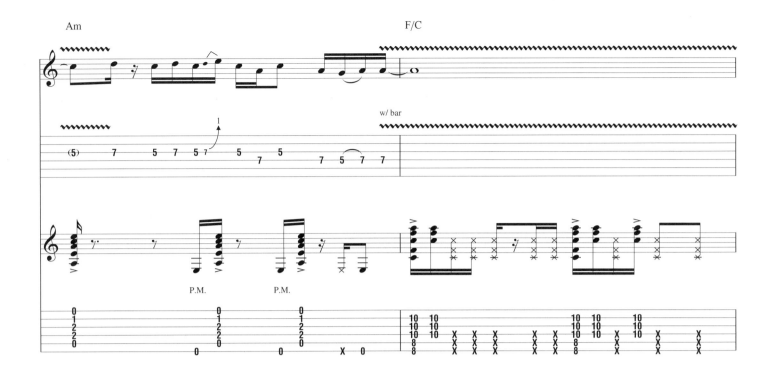

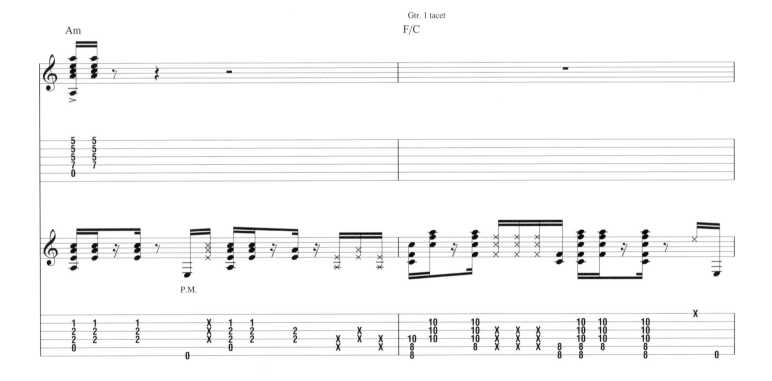

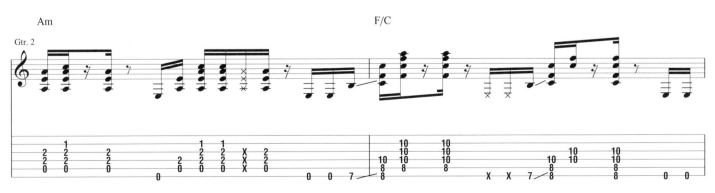

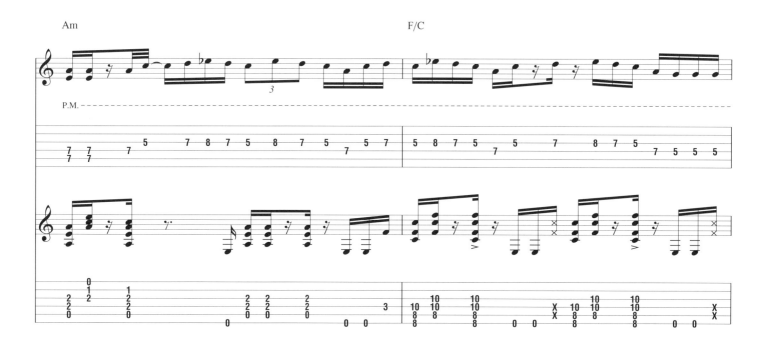

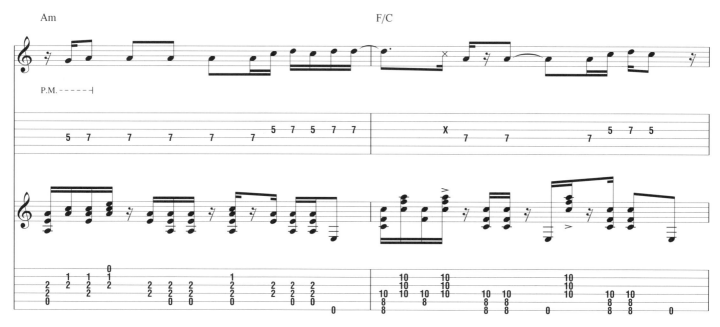

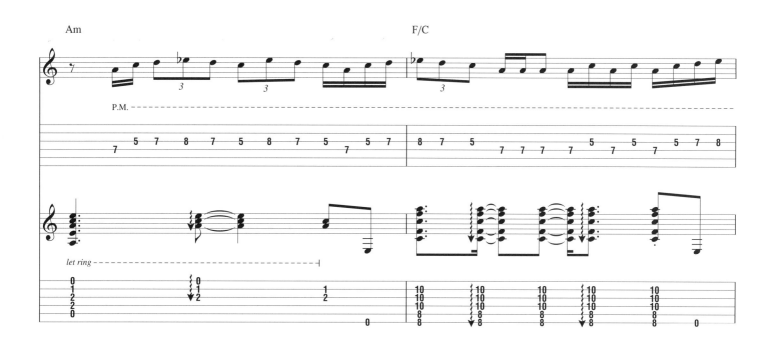

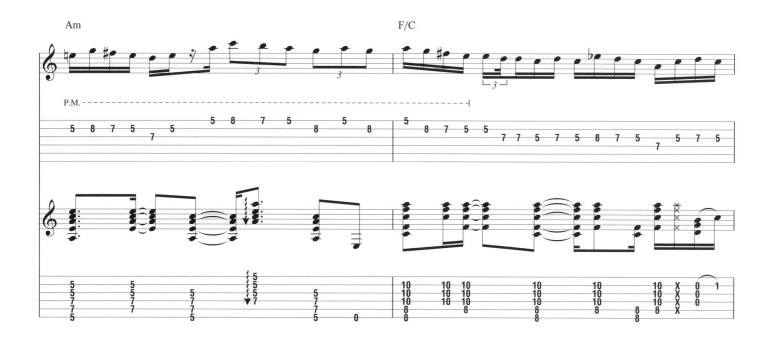

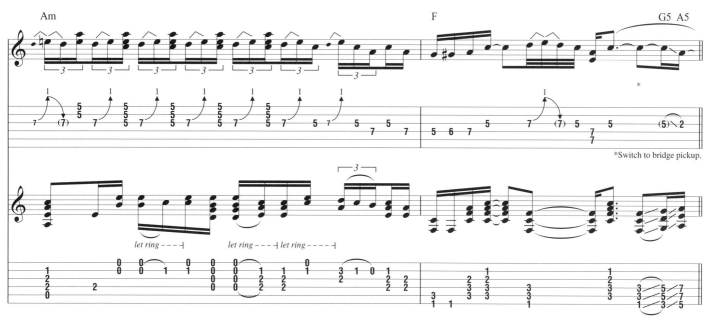

Verse

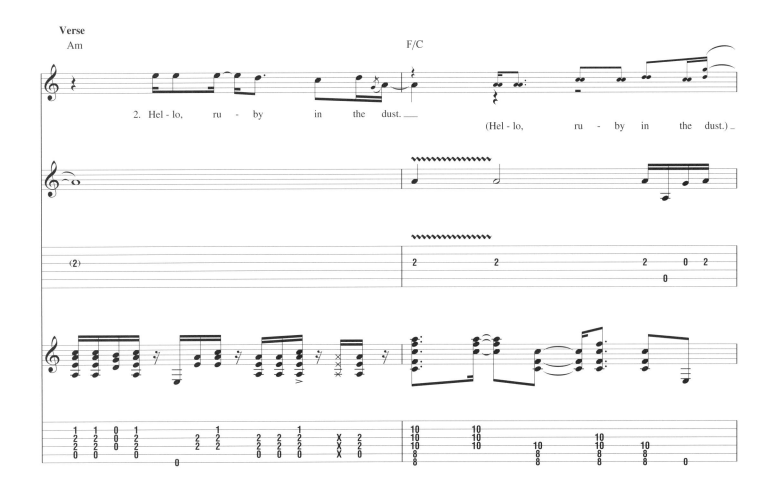

2. Hel - lo, ru - by in the dust. ___ (Hel - lo, ru - by in the dust.) ___

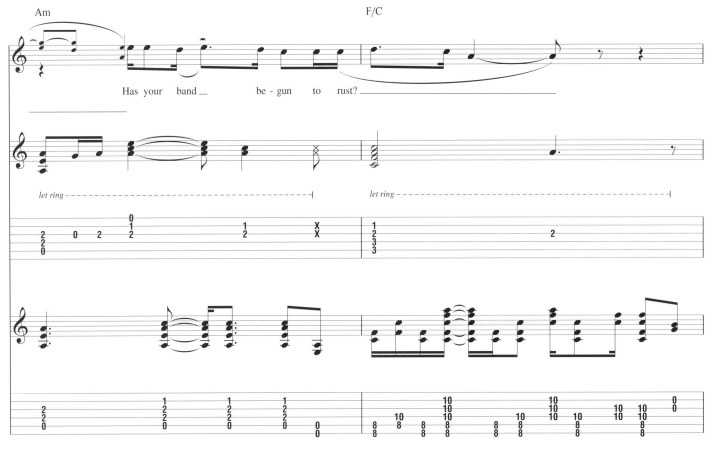

Has your band ___ be - gun to rust? ___

let ring -

let ring -

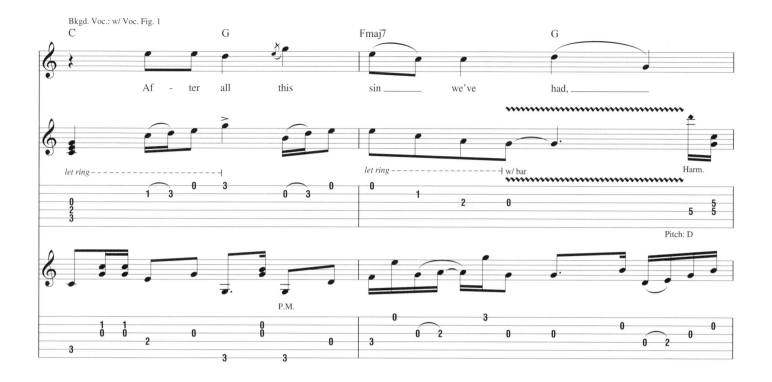

After all this sin ___ we've had, ___

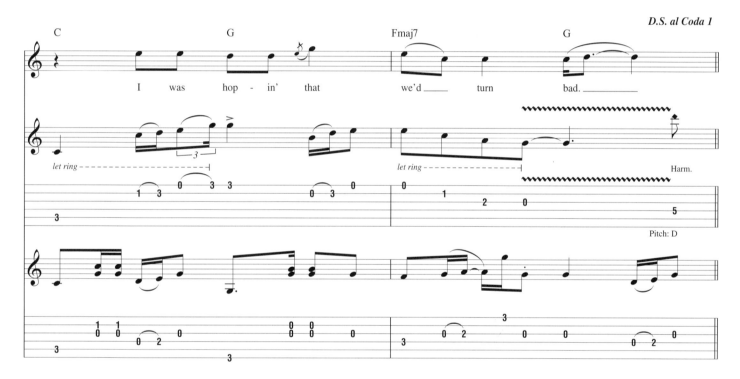

D.S. al Coda 1

I was hop-in' that we'd ___ turn bad. ___

Coda 1

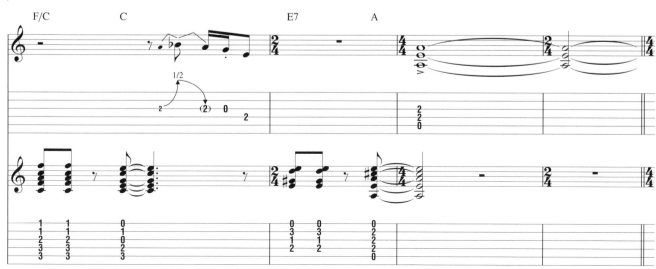

Interlude

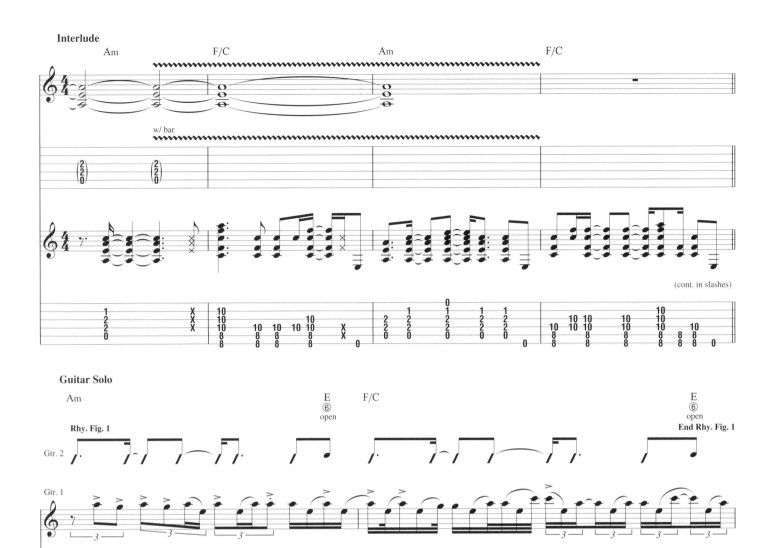

(cont. in slashes)

Guitar Solo

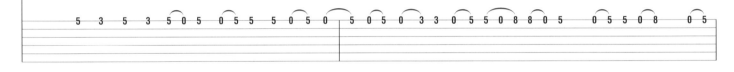

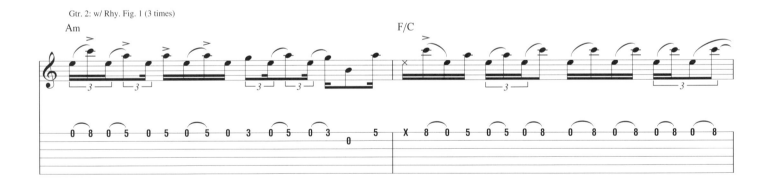

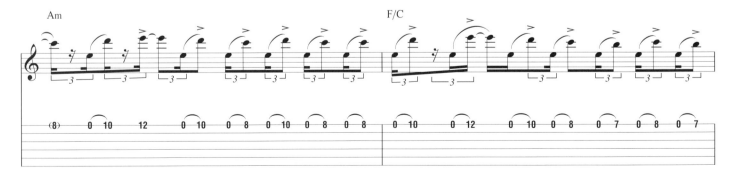

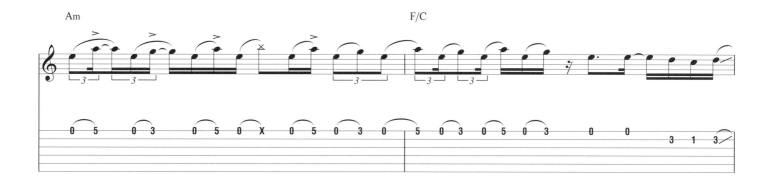

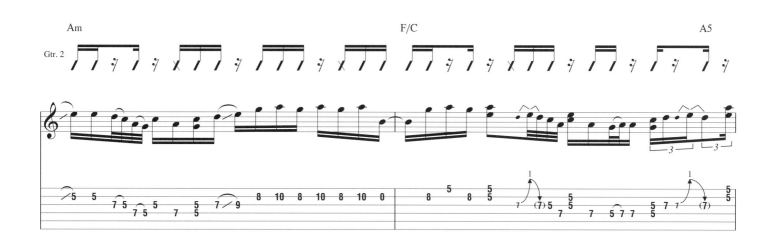

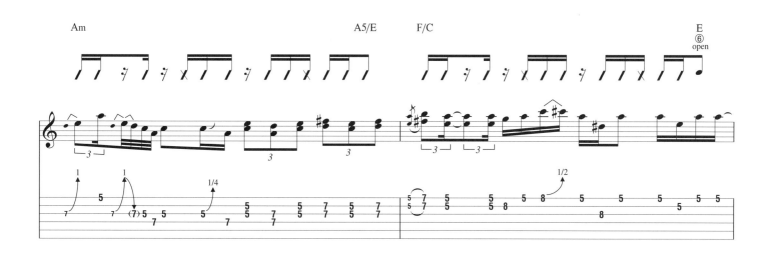

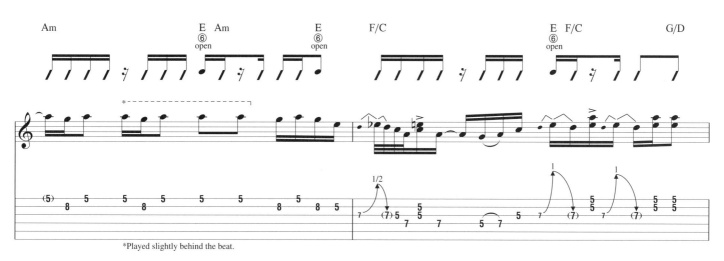

*Played slightly behind the beat.

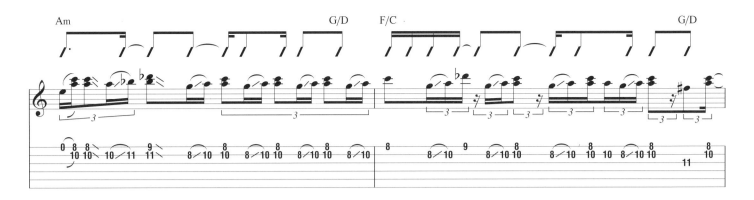

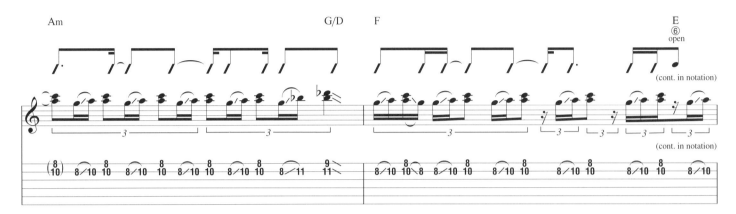

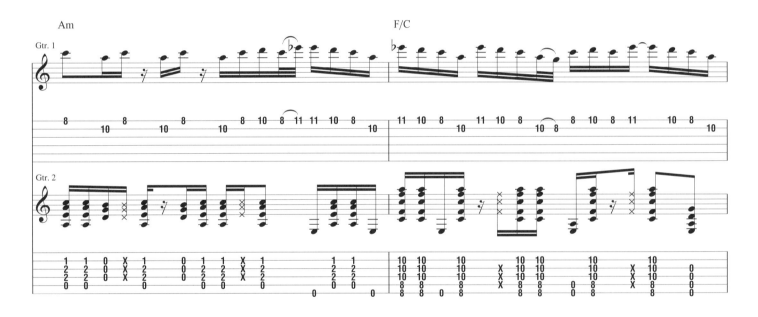

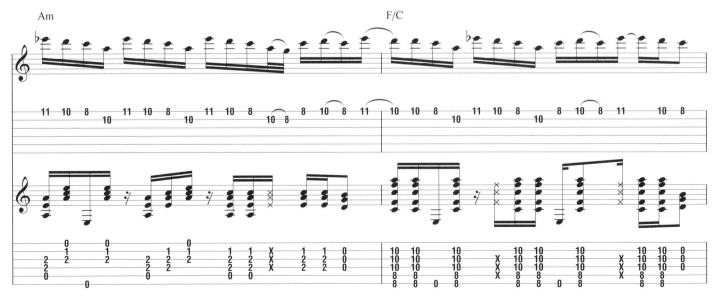

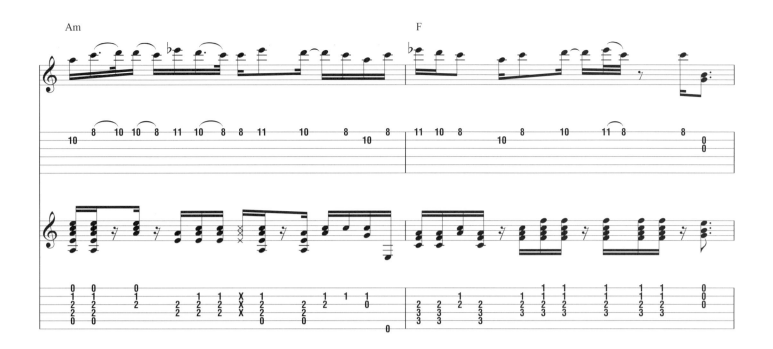

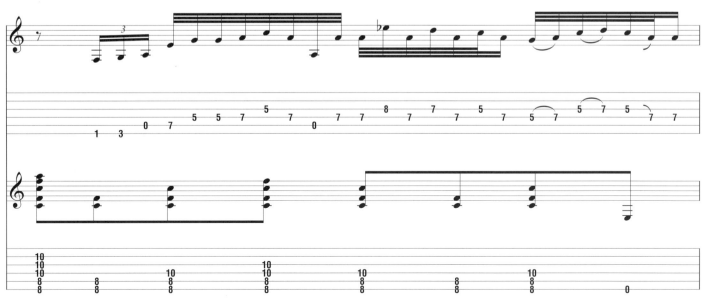

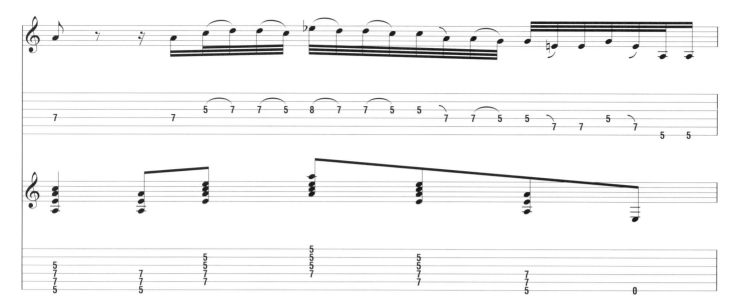

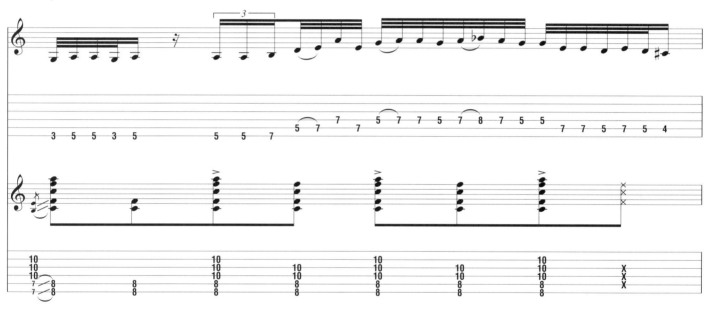

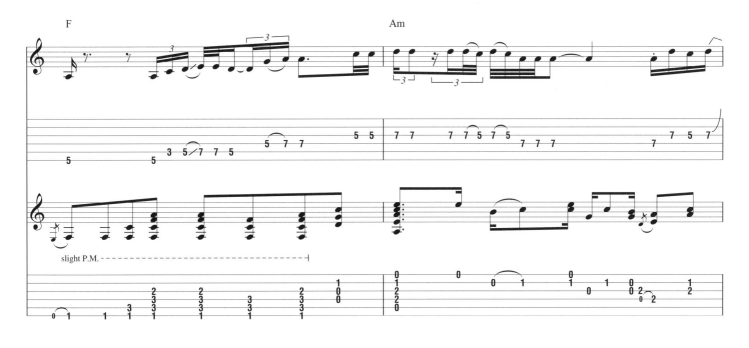

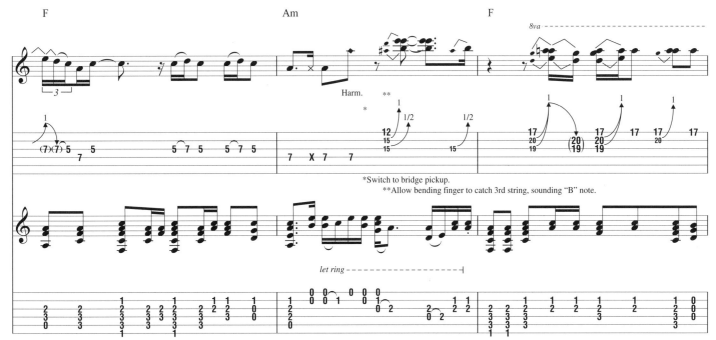

*Switch to bridge pickup.
**Allow bending finger to catch 3rd string, sounding "B" note.

***As before

Verse

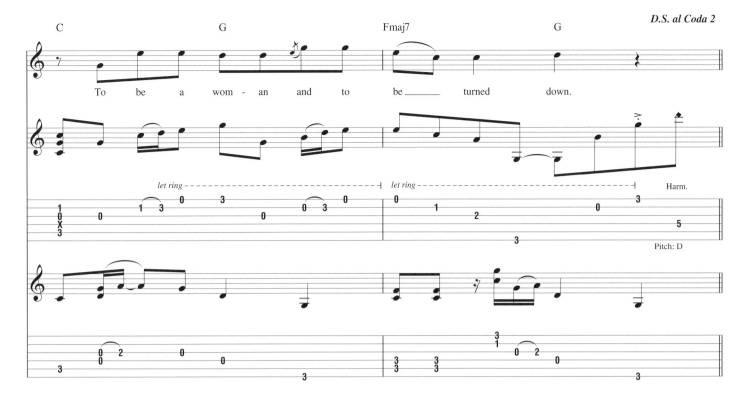

To be a wom - an and to be _____ turned down.

Coda 2

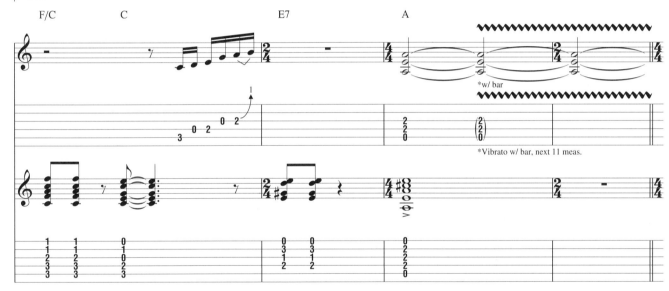

Interlude

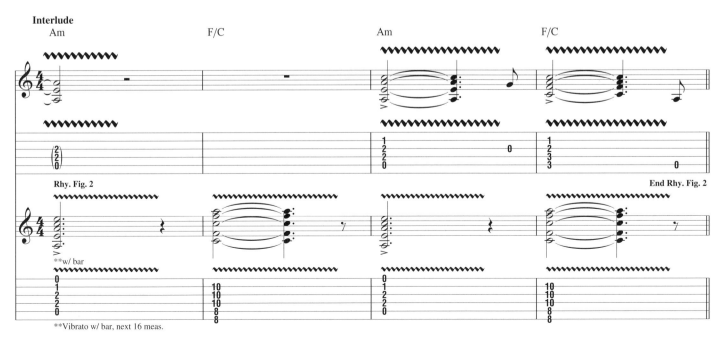

Outro-Guitar Solo

Gtr. 2: w/ Rhy. Fig. 2 (1 1/2 times)

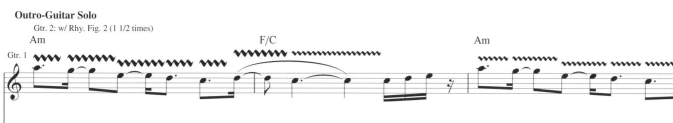

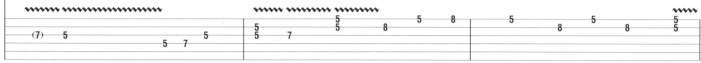

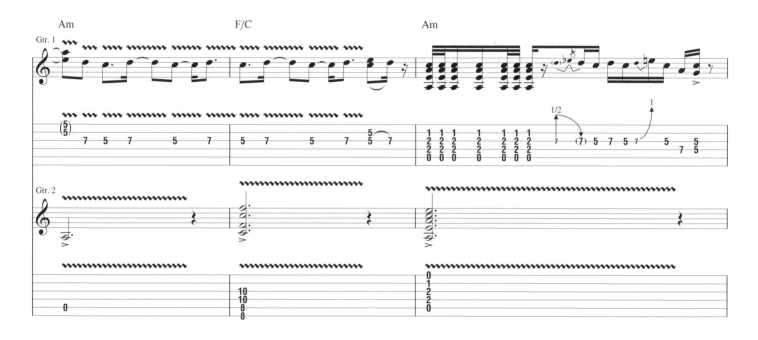

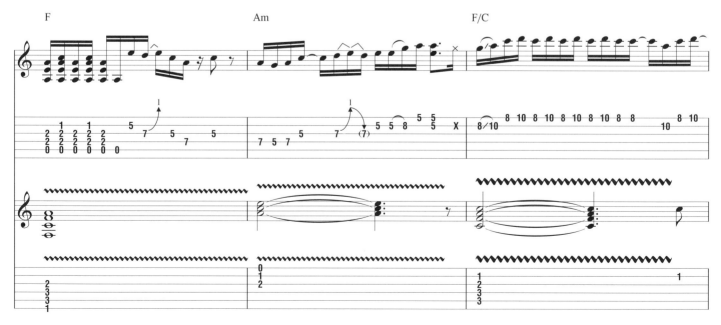

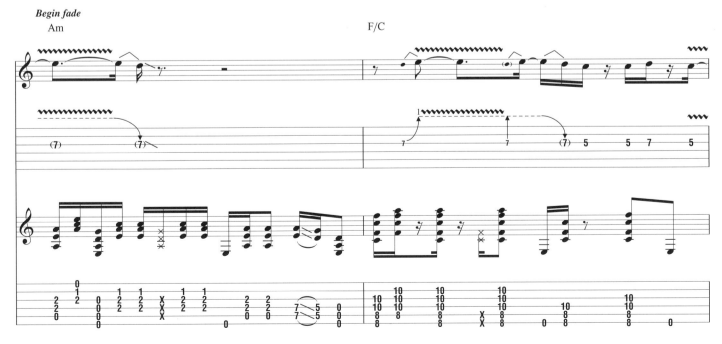

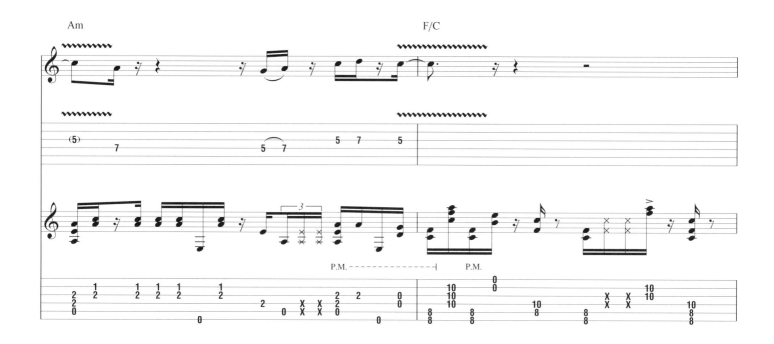

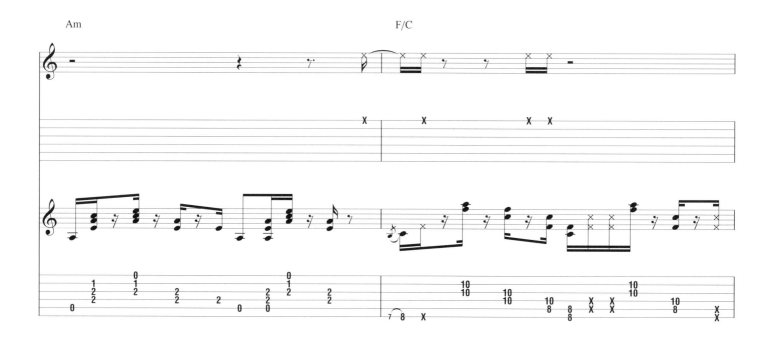

GUITAR NOTATION LEGEND

Guitar music can be notated three different ways: on a *musical staff*, in *tablature*, and in *rhythm slashes*.

RHYTHM SLASHES are written above the staff. Strum chords in the rhythm indicated. Use the chord diagrams found at the top of the first page of the transcription for the appropriate chord voicings. Round noteheads indicate single notes.

THE MUSICAL STAFF shows pitches and rhythms and is divided by bar lines into measures. Pitches are named after the first seven letters of the alphabet.

TABLATURE graphically represents the guitar fingerboard. Each horizontal line represents a string, and each number represents a fret.

HALF-STEP BEND: Strike the note and bend up 1/2 step.

WHOLE-STEP BEND: Strike the note and bend up one step.

GRACE NOTE BEND: Strike the note and immediately bend up as indicated.

SLIGHT (MICROTONE) BEND: Strike the note and bend up 1/4 step.

BEND AND RELEASE: Strike the note and bend up as indicated, then release back to the original note. Only the first note is struck.

PRE-BEND: Bend the note as indicated, then strike it.

VIBRATO: The string is vibrated by rapidly bending and releasing the note with the fretting hand.

WIDE VIBRATO: The pitch is varied to a greater degree by vibrating with the fretting hand.

HAMMER-ON: Strike the first (lower) note with one finger, then sound the higher note (on the same string) with another finger by fretting it without picking.

PULL-OFF: Place both fingers on the notes to be sounded. Strike the first note and without picking, pull the finger off to sound the second (lower) note.

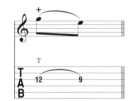

LEGATO SLIDE: Strike the first note and then slide the same fret-hand finger up or down to the second note. The second note is not struck.

SHIFT SLIDE: Same as legato slide, except the second note is struck.

TRILL: Very rapidly alternate between the notes indicated by continuously hammering on and pulling off.

TAPPING: Hammer ("tap") the fret indicated with the pick-hand index or middle finger and pull off to the note fretted by the fret hand.

NATURAL HARMONIC: Strike the note while the fret-hand lightly touches the string directly over the fret indicated.

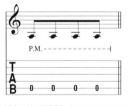

PINCH HARMONIC: The note is fretted normally and a harmonic is produced by adding the edge of the thumb or the tip of the index finger of the pick hand to the normal pick attack.

PICK SCRAPE: The edge of the pick is rubbed down (or up) the string, producing a scratchy sound.

MUFFLED STRINGS: A percussive sound is produced by laying the fret hand across the string(s) without depressing, and striking them with the pick hand.

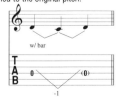

PALM MUTING: The note is partially muted by the pick hand lightly touching the string(s) just before the bridge.

RAKE: Drag the pick across the strings indicated with a single motion.

TREMOLO PICKING: The note is picked as rapidly and continuously as possible.

VIBRATO BAR DIVE AND RETURN: The pitch of the note or chord is dropped a specified number of steps (in rhythm), then returned to the original pitch.

VIBRATO BAR SCOOP: Depress the bar just before striking the note, then quickly release the bar.

VIBRATO BAR DIP: Strike the note and then immediately drop a specified number of steps, then release back to the original pitch.

PRODUCED BY
DAVID BRIGGS AND NEIL YOUNG

Neil Young - guitar • Danny Whitten - guitar
Ralph Molina - drums • Billy Talbot - bass

COVER PHOTO: FRANK BEZ
ART DIRECTION: ED THRASHER

SONGBOOK ART DIRECTION & DESIGN BY GARY BURDEN AND JENICE HEO FOR R. TWERK & CO.
SONGBOOK DESIGN BY JESSE BURDEN